THIS IS

BOAT INTERIOR CONSTRUCTION

Other titles in this series

This is Board Sailing Uwe Farke, Volker Mohle and Detlef Schröder. ISBN 0-333-36694-8

This is Boat Handling at Close Quarters Dick Everitt and Rodger Witt. ISBN 0-7136-5840-1

This is Boat Tuning for Speed, 2nd edition Fred Imhoff and Lex Pranger. ISBN 0-333-35356-0

This is Catamaran Sailing Ernst Barth and Klaus Enzmann. ISBN 0-7136-5880-0.

This is Complete Windsurfing Ulrich Stanciu. ISBN 0-85177-391-5.

This is Cruising, 2nd edition Des Sleightholme. ISBN 0-7136-5790-1.

This is Downwind Sailing John Oakley. ISBN 0-333-32214-2.

This is Fast Cruising Peter Johnson. ISBN 0-85177-347-8.

This is Looking at Sails, 2nd edition Dick Kenny. ISBN 0-7136-5800-2.

This is Practical Weather Forecasting Dieter Karnetzki. ISBN 0-7136-5701-4.

This is Racing, 2nd edition Richard Creagh-Osborne. ISBN 0-7136-5711-1.

This is Rough Weather Cruising Erroll Bruce. ISBN 0-7136-5830-4.

This is Sailing, 3rd edition Richard Creagh-Osborne. ISBN 0-7136-3392-1

This is Motor Boating Ramon Gliewe. ISBN 0-7136-3458-8

THIS IS
BOAT INTERIOR CONSTRUCTION

MICHAEL NAUJOK

Adlard Coles Nautical
London

First edition 1992
Published by Adlard Coles Nautical
an imprint of A & C Black (Publishers) Ltd
35 Bedford Row, London WC1R 4JH

Paperback edition 1998
Copyright © United Nautical Publishers SA,
Basel, Switzerland 1992

ISBN 0-7136-4954-2

Apart from any fair dealing for the purposes of
research or private study, or criticism or review,
as permitted under the Copyright, Designs and
Patents Act, 1988, this publication may be
reproduced, stored or transmitted, in any form
or by any means, only with the prior permission
in writing of the publishers, or in the case of
reprographic reproduction in accordance with
the terms of licences issued by the Copyright
Licensing Agency. Inquiries concerning
reproduction outside those terms should be sent
to the publishers at the address above.

A CIP catalogue record for this book is available
from the British Library.

Typeset in Times New Roman by
August Filmsetting, Haydock, St Helens
Printed and bound in Italy

Contents

Preface	6
Why do your own fitting out?	7
How do I choose the right boat?	8
The yacht of my choice	11
The cabin as a workshop	16
Profiled battens and fittings	22
Countersinking, screwing and plugging	26
Doors, frames and spring catches	29
Interior linings	33
Making curves and corners	38
Wood cladding for inner hull and headlinings	43
The fresh water system	46
Chart table and locker	51
Fitting out the galley	57
The saloon: lockers, bunks and table	64
Fitting out the heads	71
Finishing touches: covering the joins	77
Fitting profiled battens and panels as headlinings	81
Gas installation	86
Upholstery for comfort and style	91
Installing instruments	95
Fitting a lightning conductor	99
Soundproofing the engine compartment	101
The electrical system	103
Varnishing	106
Fitted carpets	110
Perspex doors	112
Perfection in design and colour	114
Selecting the sails	118
Laid teak decking	121
Index	135

Preface

'Learning by doing' or 'practice makes perfect' – operating on that principle I have over the past few years fitted out five yachts myself, from a small 7 metre coastal cruiser up to an 11 metre yacht.

Even if the first DIY effort didn't work out right straight away, and much of the detailed work didn't resemble boat-building, the experience and knowledge gained and the satisfactory feeling of having achieved something with my own hands mattered a great deal to me.

With the second boat things went a lot more smoothly. The experience gained and an increased tool kit contributed to its success.

This book has two objectives: to encourage the beginner (with proper planning and preparation, fitting out a boat really isn't very difficult) and to provide the experienced amateur builder with tips for optimising the results of his labours. Should you decide to undertake a fit-out, whether starting from scratch, or a partial restoration, or even just finishing off a nearly completely built yacht, take the following important tenets to heart: *never work against a deadline* and *always finish one section completely* before starting work on another. This is probably the most important knowledge I have gained from the boats I have built myself over many years, and I would urge all of you to take it on board before starting to read this book and begin 'carpentering'.

In the first part of the book I have given advice concerning selection of the right type of boat and the right materials to begin with – because choosing the right sort of hull is the beginning of the 'adventure' of DIY fitting out. The later chapters are equally applicable to fitting out a sailing yacht as a motor cruiser, since the living spaces below deck are substantially the same in both.

My special thanks go to master boatbuilder Gustav Dohse of the Hamburg Yacht Centre, who was always ready to give me advice.

Michael Naujok
1990

Why do your own fitting out?

From the point of view of the businessman who calculates value to the nearest penny, it's extremely difficult to find arguments which make working on a boat yourself look worthwhile. Proof of this is simple: if that same businessman applied his highly-qualified expertise in his spare time to providing financial advice, for instance, putting in the same amount of time, he would surely be able to make all the money necessary to buy his dream yacht. Viewed in that way, merely on the basis of saving money, doing your own fitting out would never be economically beneficial.

So why do it, if practical common sense argues against it? Some people enjoy the challenge of creating something with their own hands; they take a pride in their achievement and want to realise their own ideas. To these enthusiasts, the question of efficiency is almost irrelevant. What is important is the creative freedom inherent in doing work for yourself.

At this point I want to advise anyone against doing any building work themselves if they are thinking of doing it simply on the basis of sample calculations. They won't even get as far as the launch before suffering shipwreck. Numerous abandoned bare-hull wrecks are proof of this. However, if you see just building the boat as a labour of love, you should make the slipway, even though there will undoubtedly be ups and downs.

There is a good deal of demand nowadays for yachts more than 10 metres long which, apart from being fully seaworthy, also offer a great deal of comfort. It is particularly this size that is worth building or fitting out yourself. Recent enquiries have shown a substantial increase in the numbers of not only long-range but also long-time-live-aboard craft. A lengthy passage would be the fulfilment of a dream to many escapists and early retireds.

Years ago, the peak of this target group's ambition was a steel-hulled craft, but nowadays more and more boats have GRP or light alloy hulls. Some firms which at one time worked only with steel now do about 30 per cent of their work with light alloys; some yards have even gone over entirely to aluminium.

National and international demand for all types and sizes of boats is going to continue to grow during the coming years, and the decision whether to settle for GRP, steel or light alloy is one every owner has to make for himself. There is no clear grading of first, second or third class for these materials, although the following guidelines may help. Steel is cheaper, and can be worked even by non-experts but is heavier and rusts. Light alloy is more expensive, calls for expertise in welding it, is much lighter, does not rust, but can be destroyed by electrolysis, so light alloy hulls should preferably be acquired complete for fitting out from expert firms. Bare hulls in GRP are corrosion-proof, provide many options and, thanks to their gel coat, are in effect already 'varnished'. So for the first time fitter-out a GRP yacht offers a successful outcome with minimum difficulty.

Since almost all the major boatbuilders are thoroughly familiar with the materials, you should follow the advice of these experts even as early as the outline planning stage. The decision as to which material to use will also be affected by where you intend to sail.

Anyone unable to make up their mind whether to use GRP, steel or light alloy has a further option: building a boat with a steel hull and a light

How do you

alloy superstructure would present few problems. This solution combines great hull strength with low deck weight. And for those who love wood there is another solution: a hull of steel or light alloy with the deck and interior made of wood. This plethora of options is available only for one-offs, however. DIY builders with special woodworking skills also have a wide choice open to them, ranging from the hot or cold moulded hull to the massive mahogany shell. Generally speaking, however, sales of wooden-hulled yachts are declining.

Important decisions have to be made before building begins; in particular what size the craft will be and how much of the work you are going to do yourself. Many people discover after finishing the job that they opted for one size too small, whereas larger craft would have required only an insignificant amount of extra work, although probably quite a bit more money. You should also plan only to do work which you're confident is within your capabilities. Thus many owners have the hull built for them and carry out only the installation of the interior fittings, because building the hull from scratch is always the most difficult part of the job. DIY builders planning to tackle working with metal for the first time should obtain advice from designers with extensive experience of DIY building by owners.

If you are uncertain what route to take, get in touch with other DIY builders – there is no substitute for an exchange of experience between owners.

Choosing the right boat is often much more difficult than doing the building or fitting out yourself. Sailing as a sport is these days so multifaceted that you have to proceed systematically to arrive at the right choice. To make this decision process easier I have therefore drawn up a chart encompassing all of the main boat types. At the left-hand side is the 'crew's requirement' and at the right-hand side the boat to match it. For example: the crew (including of course the owner/skipper), after due consideration, have decided on cruising. Now the question of the type of waters to be sailed in has to be considered; inland waters (rivers, lakes etc), coastal waters or, ultimately, the open sea, because the characteristics of boats for each of these differ.

Let's assume that the skipper decides on the 'fully seaworthy' category: another decision now becomes necessary. What sort of a keel is this sea-going cruiser to have for instance? A long keel for long cruises to distant parts or a fin keel for handiness and high speed on jaunts in European waters? And how about draught? If our skipper wants not only to sail offshore but also to anchor in shallow bays, he's going to have to have a lifting keel or a keel and centreplate boat. So apart from the question of the materials, finding the right type of boat also calls for a whole host of details to be settled.

What is perhaps even more important is deciding on the size of the boat. I once coined a phrase: 'At 9.5 metres in length, comfort and convenience begin; at 10.5 metres they end'. What I meant by this was that from 9.5 metres overall length upwards all the important features such as a navigation area, galley, saloon, bunks, engine compartment, sanitary facilities and so forth for the standard crew of two to four can be fitted in. Moreover a boat of this size is still relatively easy to handle; even a small crew needs no more than muscle power to master the sails, whereas yachts way beyond the 11 metre boundary require either a lot of technology (roller-reefing, anchor winches, bow thruster etc) or the combined muscle power of a large (racing) crew.

choose the right boat?

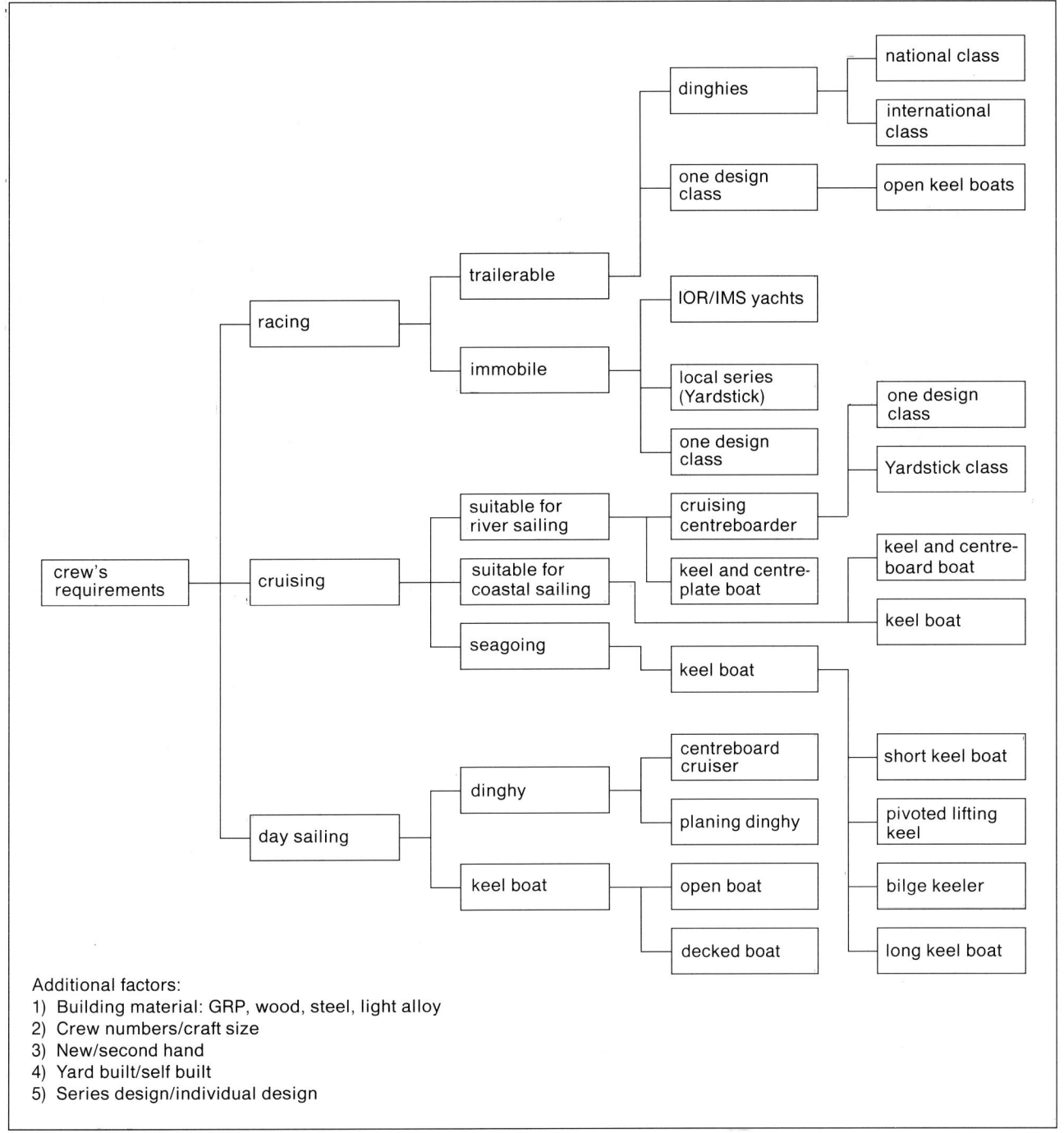

Additional factors:
1) Building material: GRP, wood, steel, light alloy
2) Crew numbers/craft size
3) New/second hand
4) Yard built/self built
5) Series design/individual design

Below, I have assembled, in a five-point programme, everything that must be attended to before even the first hammer-blow is struck.

What DIY builders produce ranges from the super-boat to the wreck which will never float with the proverbial hand's breadth of water under the keel. That explains why there is continuing heated discussion between those in favour of DIY boatbuilding and those against. Doing the work youself can, however, allow you to implement many personal preferences and to save up to 40 per cent of the average yard costs.

Rule 1: Don't overestimate your skill as a craftsman

Everyone should be sure about what they are capable of. Don't rely on the salesman's pitch which gives the impression that it's all very easy. Anyone wanting to fit out a hull from scratch should have reasonable manual dexterity, sufficient knowledge to interpret drawings, and a basically accurate assessment of their own skills – which will ensure that expert advice is sought before any problems get out of hand. More importantly, anyone intending to construct and fit out a steel hull should either be conversant with working with steel professionally or get a welding expert to carry out the structurally important work.

By contrast, even a layman can make a laminated hull given precise instructions. Anyone totally lacking boatbuilding experience would do well to start either by undertaking a very modest project himself or by gaining the necessary experience helping a friend or fellow member of a club. Anyone who takes on a project irresponsibly will certainly pay for it, either in terms of additional expenditure during the building stage or ultimately in the rough and tumble of life at sea.

Rule 2: Have a precise plan ready

Anyone who tries to make savings at the planning stage or who disregards important points is going to suffer shipwreck before the boat even gets to the launch site.

Even the choice of the type of craft has to be part of the plan; you must have a clear picture of the kind of waters in which you intend to sail and how many people would normally expect to live on board. Decide whether it is to be a keel boat, a keel and centreboard boat, or a bilge keeler, and in making your preparations also take into account the nature of the site where you are going to work. A site under cover, with heating available to keep the temperature constant, is worth aiming for. Unheated sheds during the cold season are not much better than a covering tarpaulin. And building a boat in the open is something you shouldn't even think of in northern latitudes.

Rule 3: Include every detail in your financial plan

Get hold of every available catalogue of the relevant accessory manufacturers and draw up a parts list – but list the exact prices not just approximate ones. Compare prices too – this is well worth while. And consult owners who have already fitted out a craft of this type; they will be able to give you not only prices but also advice about timescales and possible difficulties, and maybe tips about shortcuts. Insurance firms or providers of building plans will almost always have figures to hand as well; make full use of their experience.

Rule 4: Work accurately and cleanly

There is as yet no technical supervisory authority for vessels, so you yourself are totally responsible for the craft which you are laboriously putting together bit by bit. Botched work can show up either as a door that jams or as a boat that sinks. Always keep in touch with the experts, or with the manufacturer. Where dimensions are given, stick to these precisely. Calculated ballast proportions are obligatory, and changes on the basis of personal deliberations are not allowed.

The yacht of my choice

Many a DIY builder has thrown in the towel halfway through the job because of growing dissatisfaction with the work, so if the launch date starts to loom threateningly it is better to omit some small unit (for example the galley) entirely for the time being rather than rush the job and have to do it all again later.

Rule 5: Base your project on a proven design

Above all choose a boat which 'looks right' from the drawings; preferably produced by a well-known designer. If it looks right as drawn, you can also count on an attractive hull shape with harmonious lines. Only a boat appealing to the eye with the best of sailing qualities is worth the effort, gives enduring pleasure, and gives you a chance of a reasonably satisfactory price should you want to sell it later. Your safest course will be to select a design for which these positive criteria have long been established.

In my search for my 'dream boat' I was faced with a vast range on offer and endured the proverbial 'embarrassment of choice'. What I was looking for was a sailing yacht with particularly good, even sportsboat-like, sailing qualities. On the one hand it should need no more than two to crew it, but if necessary it should provide living space for up to four or six. My choice of boat was the CB-33 – a Carl Beyer design – based on the following characteristics: harmonious lines above and below the waterline, a tall, flexible rig with a large sail area, a deep lead keel for maximum stability and, last but not least, sandwich construction using balsawood. The small Swedish Satas yard (a permanent work-force of three brothers) while not producing large numbers does produce high quality. I decided on the so-called 'sail-away' version, which means bare inside, finished outside.

This degree of completion (including main bulkheads and engine) makes it possible for the new owner to sail his acquisition home 'under its own steam', so saving the cost of transport. The boat includes sails in the list price.

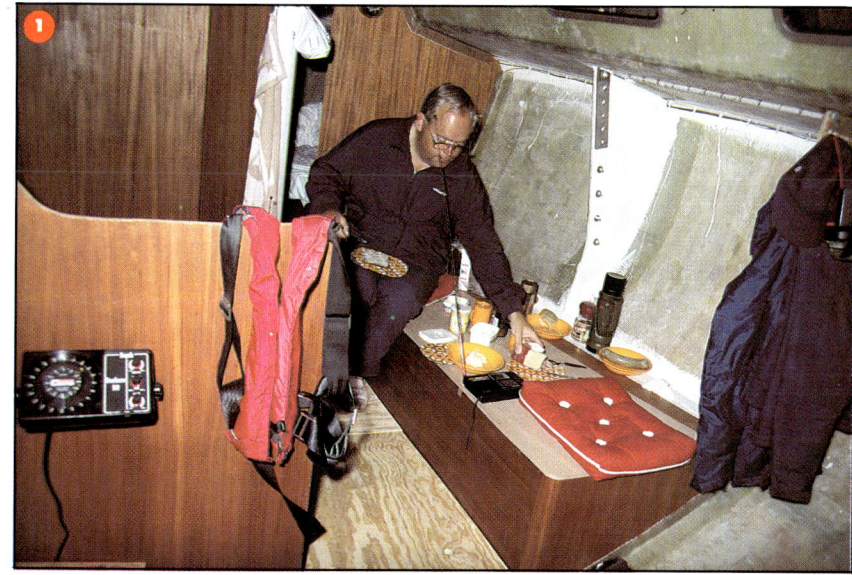

1 CB-33 beforehand: equipment essential for the initial passage has been fitted. The main bulkheads, a plain plywood temporary sole, and the bases of the bunks have been roughly put together.

2 CB-33 afterwards: some 1000 hours of work have been put in and the interior has taken shape. The galley is port side forward. At the saloon table there is ample room for four people.

3 CB-33 close-hauled: the tall mast carries about 60 square metres of sail close-hauled, so good sailing qualities are guaranteed even when there is little wind.

This book is designed to allow all the jobs demonstrated to be carried out in almost any other type of boat. The dimensions may change, of course, but the basic skills and working techniques are universally applicable.

Technical data

Length overall:	9.96 m
Beam (maximum):	3.38 m
Draught:	1.85 m
Displacement:	4.1 tonnes
Lead ballast:	1.78 tonnes
Waterline length:	8.20 m
Mast height:	15.6 m
Mainsail:	29.6 sq m
Genoa I:	34.2 sq m
Genoa II:	28.5 sq m
Cruising jib:	22.4 sq m
Engine:	Yanmar 2GM 18 bhp/3600 rpm
Designer:	Carl Beyer

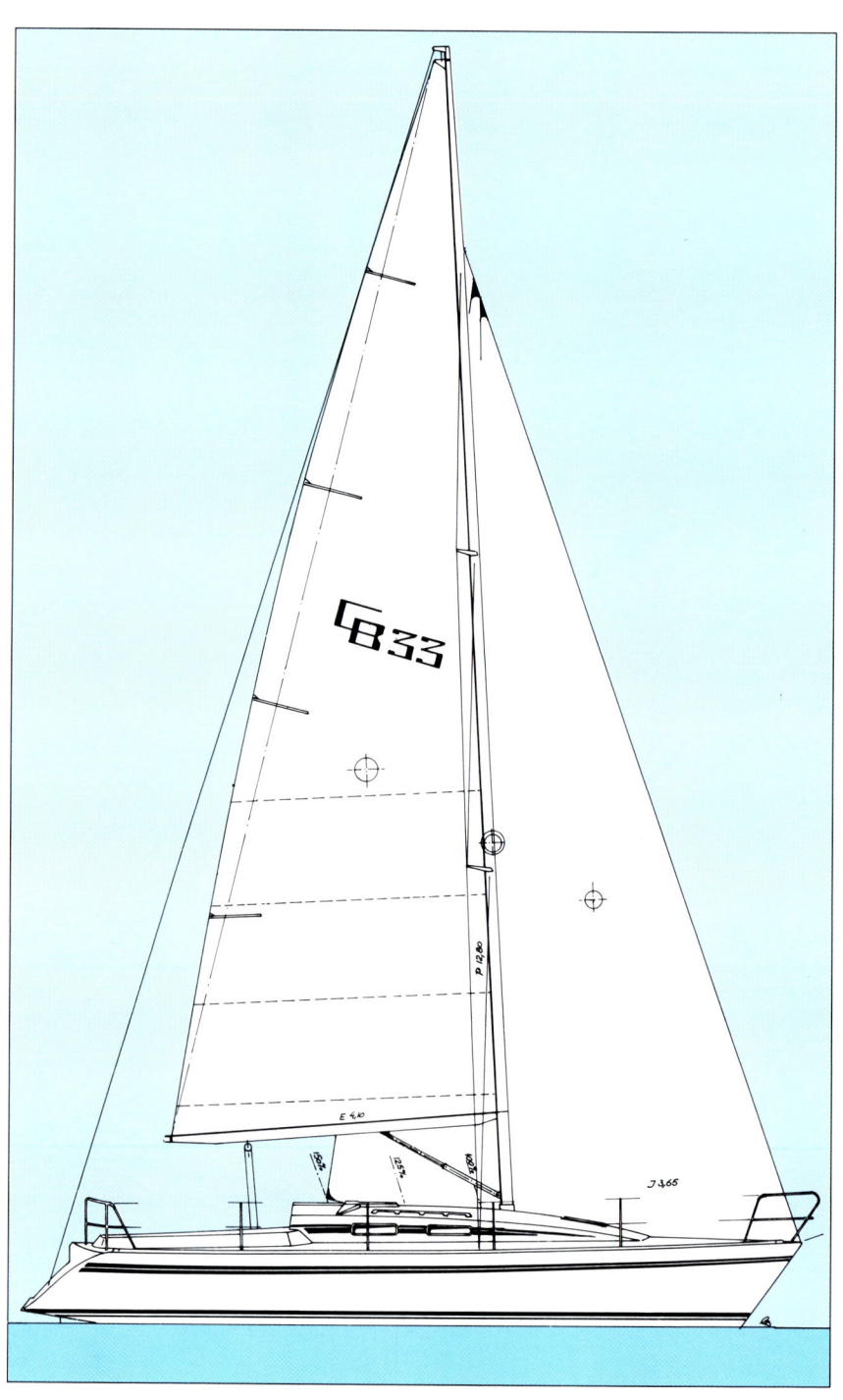

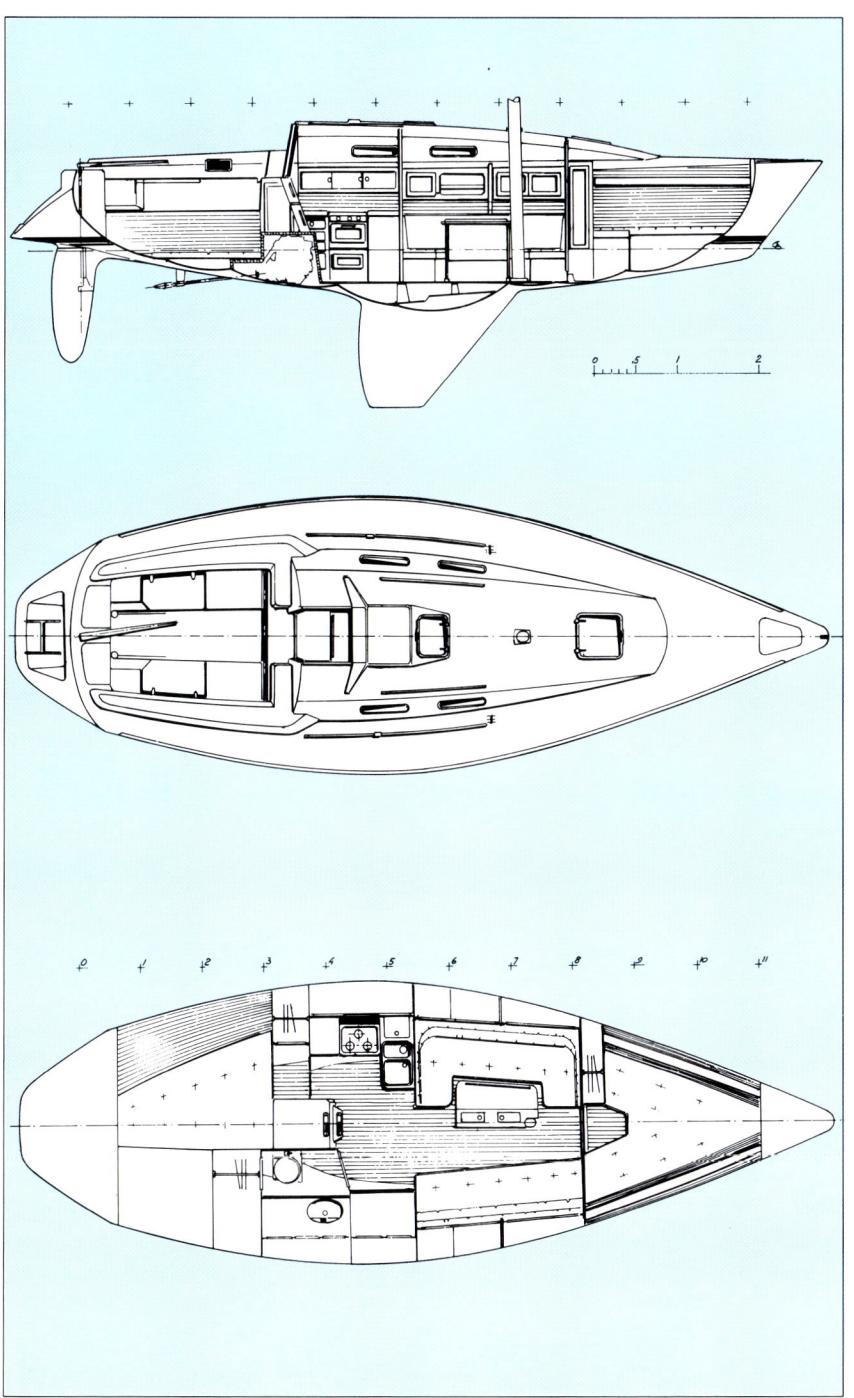

Elevation, plan views

The CB-33 is a fin keel boat with a deep draught keel and a partially balanced fin rudder. The internal subdivision I have left substantially as designed by the yard, but I did alter the saloon arrangement: the table is different, the seat backrests slope more, there are open shelves, etc. Alterations were also made in the galley: the working surface was raised (to make room for a refrigerator under the sink and to make it easier to work standing upright). Also there is more room all round the gimballed cooker, for ease of cleaning.

The cabin as a workshop

This chapter is intended to create the right preconditions for satisfactorily fitting out a boat yourself. It deals with what tools are going to be needed and how the cabin is prepared to act as a workshop. Sensible investments now will be repaid many times later.

I built my first sailing yacht in a meadow under a tarpaulin – without electricity. The work, and the result, was often highly depressing since even with proper planning and preparation, lack of power tools can only be made good by slow and painstaking manual effort. Now, twenty years later, I would never dream of working that way. For one thing, my standards for my own work are much higher; for another, power tools have become readily available. Similarly, small hand tools have become much better in recent years without any substantial increase in price. The many large firms of builders' merchants have ensured a readily available supply of these.

For what is now my fourth go at fitting out a sailing yacht I have a set of tools which while not lavish does include all the really necessary equipment and special tools – always with 'working on board' in mind, so everything has to be neat and compact. As a DIY-er you can forget all about a circular saw bench or a truing table. With proper planning, you can get by without.

In this listing I am only going to include the most important special tools, because I think it fair to assume that any hobbyist contemplating fitting out a boat will already possess hammers, screwdrivers, pliers and suchlike.

1 Jig saw: this is probably the most important tool of all for a woodworker. Cutting speed should be infinitely adjustable, and the saw should have a chip blower to remove the chips from where you are cutting – otherwise you will quickly run out of puff.

2 Grinding head: this attachment for an electric drill is used for sharpening twist drills, shortening screws, opening-out round apertures, fairing GRP edges and a host of other things.

3 Electric drills and screwdriver: you need at least two or three electric drills to avoid spending much time exchanging drill bits, countersinks and milling cutters. Furthermore, I recommend a battery-driven screwdriver with a rapid-charging unit. Check that the tool has a forwards-backwards switch that is quick to operate.

4 Diamond wheel: this attachment is also simply gripped in the drill chuck. This grinding wheel, which scarcely glazes and has a long working life, is excellent for smoothing laminate joins and smoothing/levelling GRP edges.

5 Disc or angle grinder with table: no DIY boat-builder should lack this small, but nevertheless enormously important, disc grinder. Excellent for grinding edges, mitres and angles. If you use it to make mitred-corner frames they will be a really good fit.

6 90-degree countersink: all countersunk-head screws need a recess for the head if they are to sit properly. Don't use a cheap tool; it's more likely to tear the wood than to cut it neatly.

7 Hole saw: an important tool for circular apertures, whether for ventilation, taking hoses through or just for holding glasses. A good hole-cutting tool is important; don't pick the cheapest type which is used to cut GRP – it will quickly give up the ghost. It will also tear wood and plywood if not used carefully.

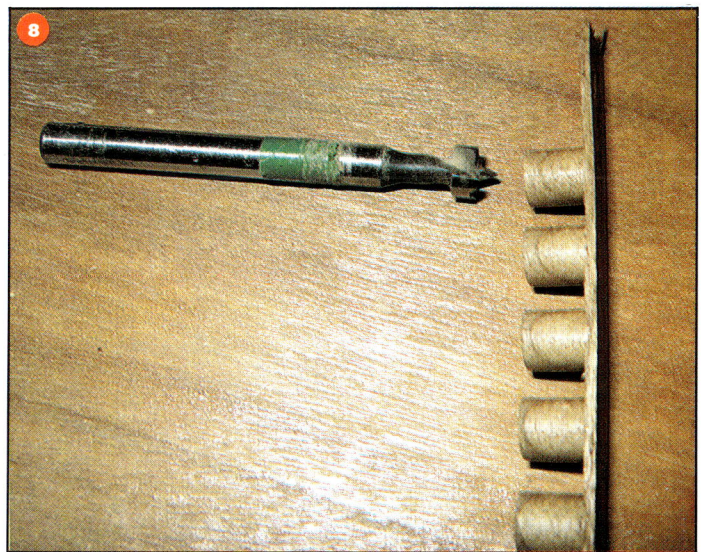

8 Plug hole drill: this special tool is indispensable for drilling blind holes to be sealed later using wooden plugs. Pick a really good one, because with a 10 metre yacht there may be several hundred of these plugs.

9 Drawing instruments: steel set square with wooden stop face, steel rule and metal tape measure are an absolute must. Without these three tools, dimensionally accurate work is impossible. The tape measure should be suitable for internal measurements and be at least three metres long.

10 Screw cramps: as necessary for the DIY fitter-out as the anvil for the smith. No cramps – no joy. The motto here: the more, the better. There should be at least ten on board, if possible differing in size.

11 Spirit level: without this, no aligning. Using it presupposes the hull is lying absolutely level in both directions!

12 Mitre jig: wooden ones are no good; light alloy ones just acceptable. Mitre-box saws with column guides, which still cut a true angle after much use, are better value.

13 Cylindrical milling cutter: these small extra bits for drills are indispensable for dressing, enlarging and fairing edges, particularly where there is no room for larger tools.

14 Bevelled milling cutter: these drill inserts are needed for GRP regions awkward to reach with a drill; for instance, for apertures for hoses down amongst the bottom frames.

15 Scissors and craft knife: necessary for working with thin materials such as templates, veneers, cladding material, cardboard, carpet and the like.

In setting up the cabin as a workshop you should proceed as follows: first lay a stout temporary floor, able to stand being drilled into accidentally from time to time. Suitable materials are sheets of unpolished plywood or hardboard. Lighting is provided by one or two deckhead-mounted 60 watt fluorescent lights plus one or two lamps on leads with pearl bulbs (100 watt) which are used as necessary. Power is supplied via two five-outlet multi-point connectors.

To provide a workbench you put up the galley structure roughly, and on top of this lay a sheet of plywood, 16 millimetres thick, as a work surface. Thus you get a work table, to which you can even fasten the angle grinder. The two saloon bunks, not yet fitted with the fiddles for the sea-cushions that come later, can serve as additional workbenches.

Profiled battens and fittings

Part of making a good job of fitting out a boat is the correct choice of matching profiled battens, strips and fittings. The woodworking trade and joineries stock a wide range, and you can also have battens specially made to measure should you require them.

As an amateur boatbuilder you are able to do a lot of things yourself, but precision cutting and milling of battens should be left to the professional. He has seasoned wood, profiling machines and the experience to make these parts well. I would never recommend economising in this field, because it is the battens that give the finished appearance to a yacht. If these trimmings are irregular or split it ruins the appearance.

If you are going to order battens, then before doing so make as accurate as possible a list of your requirements. It is always better to meet all of these with one order, because that gives you a reasonable assurance that you will get battens that are all the same in texture and colour. Order an extra metre or so to allow for faults or errors.

1 Profiles galore. This is a selection from a joinery firm which has specialised in the field of DIY supplies. Almost everything can be obtained in either teak or mahogany, and of course other woods by special request.

2 The profiled battens for a double sliding door. The batten with the shallow grooves is for the bottom; that with the deep grooves for the top. The doors can be easily lifted out.

3 Four types of corner. On the left, two examples for outside edges; on the right, two for inside. Batten size can be varied to match the size of the part for which it is intended.

4 These three battens are suitable, amongst other things, for concealing pipes or electric cables where these would show. The bottom left batten can also be suitable for door and door-frame all-round edging.

5 Cross-section of a teak rubbing strake. The shallow groove in the underside provides the so-called drip edge; this prevents water from the deck running back to and down the hull, and leaving dirty streaks.

6 The round bar is available in many sizes for curtain rails, clothes rails in cupboards and so on. It is usually available in diameters ranging from 10 to 30 millimetres.

7 Edging strips for treadboards, table tops and lids. Your basic rule should be: a batten is better a bit too thick than too thin. Edgings that are too narrow can be disfiguring. If you're not quite sure, try various thicknesses – it's worth it.

8 Decorative strips as edging for doors and lids. These are glued on, and if necessary screwed on from behind. Do take care that the glue does not squeeze out at the front, as it is difficult to remove glue stains.

9 Treadboards. These hefty battens are very good for companionways. The milled grooves make them very safe for stepping on to.

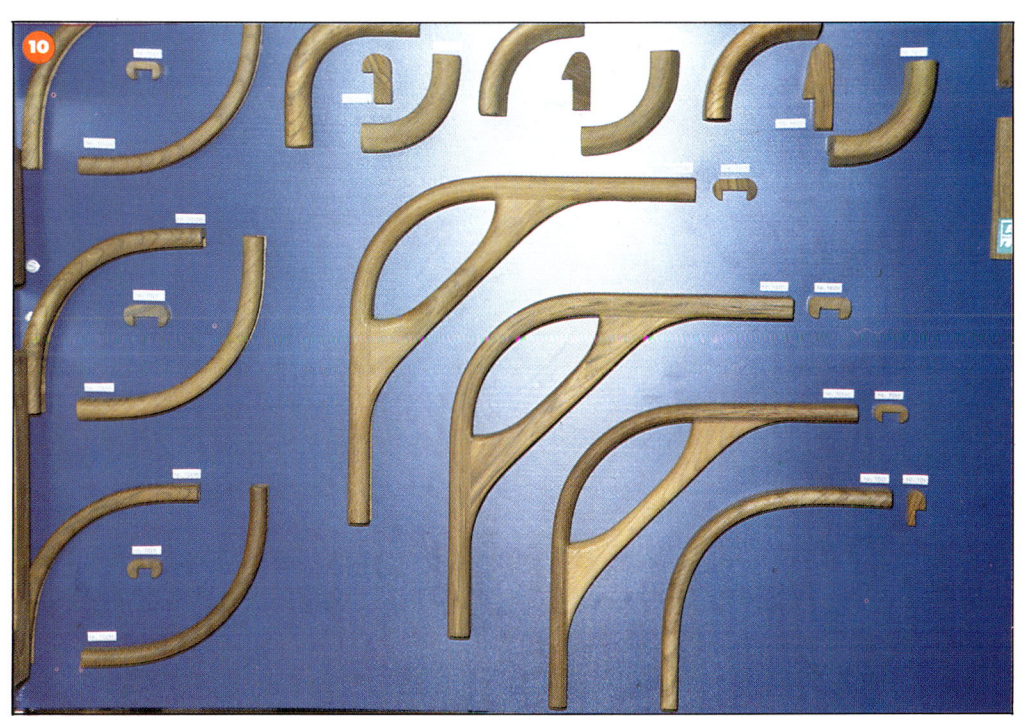

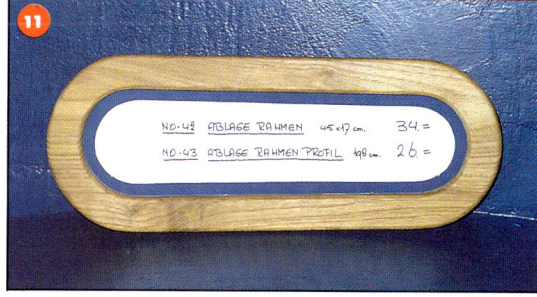

10 These handrails can be obtained in finished condition from the trade. Usually made to suit plywood panels 12 millimetres thick.

11 Ready-made wooden window frames can also usually be obtained. Making them yourself is not impossible, but very difficult.

12 A selection of handles and finger-ring collars. Fitting something like this enhances the appearance of a yacht – it gives a professional look.

Countersinking, screwing and plugging

An important and endlessly recurring task when fitting out a boat using wood is the filling-in of screw holes with small round wooden plugs. For a 10 metre yacht, several hundred will be needed.

Nothing is more irritating in a boat with wooden furnishings than the sight of shiny stainless steel screw heads – yet, sadly, with modern series construction the expertly inserted plug is becoming more and more of a rarity. Without it, a yacht simply does not have that well-finished look. The reason for omitting them is obvious: inserting, cutting back and sanding these small cylindrical pieces of wood is something that can only be done by hand and requires a lot of time and skill.

There are, of course, parts of a yacht where plugs have to be dispensed with for constructional reasons; for example very thin strips and access panels that have to be taken up again from time to time in order to run new cables or carry out inspections. Instead of using stainless steel screws where the fitting of plugs is impracticable, you should use brass ones that match the colour of the wood more closely.

Plugs can be made from any of the usual woods or bought ready-made. You can choose between 8, 10 and 12 millimetres diameter, depending on the size of the screw head. Experience indicates that you can get by pretty well with just using 10 millimetre plugs throughout. An advantage is that you need only one drill and one size of plug.

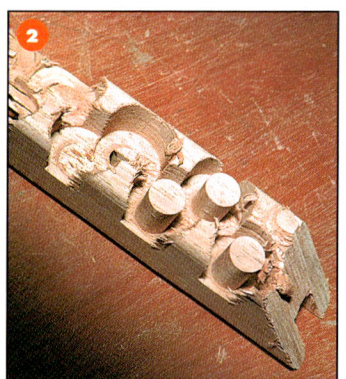

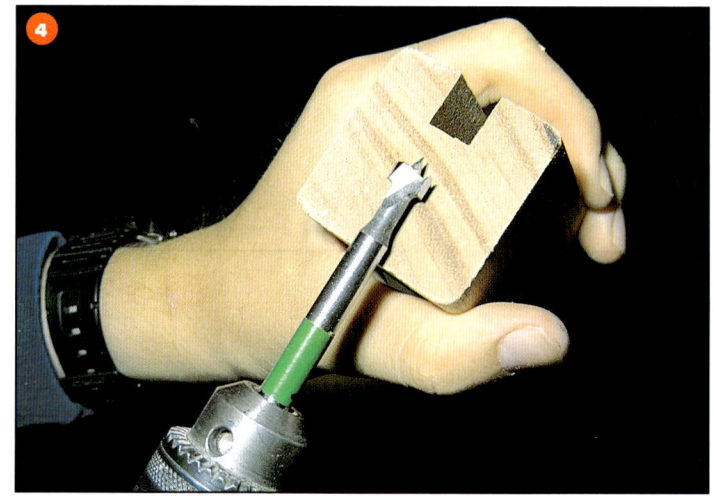

1 Bare screw heads: unfortunately a detail that occurs more and more often in series-built boats. To save time and money when completing the interior of a boat, battens, handrails and panel joins are simply screwed up; the bare Phillips screw head remains visible for ever.

2 'Home-made' plugs: plugs can easily be cut out from wood offcuts, using a trepanning drill. What you do need for this, of course, is a stable pillar drill. You also have to pay attention to the colour and the run of the grain of the wood. It is vital that you cut at right angles to the annual rings so that the plug can later be shortened 'slice by slice'.

3 Plugs from the trade: to begin with, buy just a couple to try them out. If the diameter and colour are right (mahogany varies in colour from batch to batch), you can buy larger quantities. Check that the grain runs the same way in each one and that the surface is smooth. Should the plugs have been cut out with a blunt tool, their surface will be rough and they are difficult to insert.

4 The plug hole drill: this special tool is obtainable from the trade. Operate it with high revs and low speed of advance, and make sure the chips can come out freely. When drilling deep blind holes, pull the drill out frequently and remove the chips. Since wood is a poor conductor of heat, you have to do this to save the drill from annealing and becoming soft. When drilling blind holes, always use the plug hole drill first and then cut the hole through for the screw. If you do it the other way, the centring point of the plug hole drill has no wood to hold it – the drill will wobble and tear the edges of the hole.

5 Wood screw: generally in a boat you should use stainless steel screws. In certain special situations, brass ones may be used but they tend to shear off when tightened in hardwood. When using fat screws (diameter 6 millimetres plus) pre-drilling is essential as the wood is liable to split. Furthermore, you should always use Phillips screws – they make it almost impossible for the screwdriver to slip, particularly if you use a power tool.

6 Inserting the plug: all plugs, even long ones, are always fixed in with waterproof glue. The slim nozzle of the glue bottle is used to get glue into the drilling, but not as here – shown as a bad example – in excess. The glue squeezed out must all be removed carefully, because if left, it would show up when varnished over later (though scarcely visible until then).

7 Getting the plug in right: this plug is right – colour, run of the grain and gluing are all as they should be. When hammering the plug in, the change in the sound tells you that it has butted on the screw head. Don't hammer it in too hard or you will damage the wood. Make sure that the plug does not tilt when being hammered in or you get an oval plug hole.

8 Trimming the plug: once the glue has hardened properly, the plug is trimmed in slices with a sharp chisel, angled edge down. Don't apply the blade at the batten surface level straightaway, since the fibres may not always run horizontally; this could lead to the plug shearing off below that level. You would then have to laboriously drill it out and replace it with a larger one.

9 Wrong use: never apply the chisel with the angled edge upwards, as shown here. The blade is dragged downwards and cuts off too much of the plug. All your preparatory work is wasted.

10 Smoothing-in: the last part of the job consists of going over the plug top with fine sandpaper wrapped around a wooden or cork block, moving along the grain, until the plug is smooth and flush with the surroundings. Any traces of glue must first be removed.

11 End result: the work has been done well and the grain runs the right way, but the plug is a bit too light in colour. The only way to get it right is by trial and error.

12 False start: the plug hole was not started in quite the right place. You are unlikely to be able to sand away the recess left by this false start and it will remain visible as an annular groove.

Doors, frames and spring catches

Doors are particularly essential for athwartship stowage, otherwise the contents will fall out when the boat heels. In this section you will discover how to make a professional job of a sturdy and elegant door.

One of the most time consuming jobs when fitting out a boat is making the many small locker and cupboard doors, because this has to be real precision work. Any mistake shows up immediately, so allow plenty of time for door making – even just one door a day is a respectable rate of working.

Before you start doing the work, make an overall plan for the saloon, because a good match between the individual doors is important. That means aiming at a certain symmetry and balance. Once you have decided on a certain pattern of door, you have to use this throughout the craft to give a uniform appearance.

To make the job easier, you can make doors larger than the door opening. These will then hide any constructional errors, since they overlap the opening. The disadvantage of this is that such surface-mounted doors are usually quite flimsy and have only an overlapping edge band and no rigid frame.

In contrast to those mentioned above, the doors described in detail here have to be made absolutely accurately, as otherwise the gaps between door and frame will not be exactly parallel. But the extra work is worthwhile – the door sticks out far less from the panel.

It should also be noted that these doors are made from the panels cut out of the cupboard front to provide the openings, which means absolutely matching grain and colour. As soon as you have cut out the panels you should mark them, to be able to put them back later as doors with the grain running the same way.

1 When you have finished inserting the floor of the locker, you fit the front panel with the appropriate door opening and glue and screw it in place. The opening should be central in the panel.

2 Next, the upper and lower frame strips are cut to length with mitred ends and inserted – without glue since both are going to have to be taken out again later.

3 Using the two long strips, you can establish the exact length of the short right-hand one. The simplest way of doing this is, first of all, to cut it roughly to length, hold it in position, mark it and use the angle disc to grind it to exactly the right length. The fit is checked by inserting the three strips – bottom first, then right-hand, then top. Check that the mitred edges fit together precisely.

4 The fourth strip can only be inserted if *one* leg of the 'U' is cut away, since it has to be pushed in from the front. The leg is cut off either with a saw or a chisel.

5 This is what that strip must look like before insertion. The leg has been removed right down to the bottom of the U-groove. If necessary, use glasspaper to get the surface level (original shape in the background).

6 Before finally inserting the strips, all contact surfaces – including the end faces – are coated with waterproof glue. Remove immediately any glue which has squeezed out as it will cause spots when varnished.

7 Having made the frame, you now make the door/flap. Here again, the edging strips are cut to the right length and checked against the door panel. When the glue-coated strips have been fitted, adhesive tape holds them in position.

8 Should the strips have been milled unevenly, they have to be positioned correctly by means of a cramp. However it is unusual for such 'brute force' to be necessary if the grooves in the strips have been milled cleanly. You should let the supplier of the strip have a sample of the plywood, or order ply and strips from the same source.

9 Using the angle grinder, the corners of the door are rounded lightly. Follow up by hand with glasspaper (about 200 grain) until you get to the same curvature as the strip edges.

10 When you've finished the door leaf, you mark the finger hole on the outer face. The distance from the upper edging strip must be such that there is just room for the flange of the hole edging ring.

11 The hole is made with the hole saw, working from *both* sides so as to get clean edges on both. Be careful not to tilt the saw while drilling, otherwise the hole will become too large.

12 Since the wood (edging) rings as a rule are not exactly round, you get ugly gaps in the back face.

These are first filled with waterproof glue and while this is still soft, mahogany chippings are pressed into it. When the glue has hardened, the surface can be sanded level and the only sign of the gap is that the wood looks a bit darker.

13 You can improve things in the same way if, for instance, mitred edges don't quite meet. However the gap must not be more than a millimetre wide.

14 This gap is just narrow enough for the glue/chippings treatment. Any wider, and it would be better to cut a fresh strip.

15 When the door is finished, screw the strap hinge into the opening. To get its position right, hold a length of strip against it as a guide. Using an auger, pre-drill for every screw.

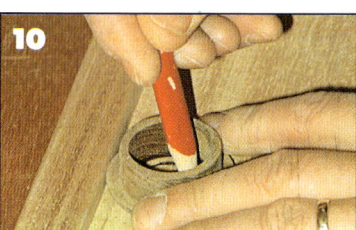

16 The correct lateral position of the door must be marked accurately because it has to be open for the hinge to be screwed to it. Initially, screw in only two screws, close the door and check that the gap between door and frame is the same on both sides.

17 The spring catch is fitted slightly off-centre because that makes it easier to use. It should be mounted to bring the hook level with the edge of the door.

18 The counterpart of the spring catch is screwed to a small block of wood fastened to the back of the frame with waterproof glue. Its lateral position is established by measurement.

19 The door is finished. The gap between leaf and frame is the same all round, the edging strips are flush – door and frame form one harmonious unit.

Interior linings

Nowadays vinyl sheet is almost one of the standard materials for fitting out boats. In this chapter we show you how to deal with it expertly – though you won't get away entirely without sticky fingers!

Synthetic interior linings found in most commercially built yachts have an attractive finish, but where there is no such lining the exposed laminate surfaces have to be faced.

Vinyl sheet is available for facing; it can be wiped clean and stretches well. The material I have used was very pleasant to work with, and had a high degree of stretchability; this is an important feature as flat surfaces are rarely found in a boat.

Colour and surface finish is a matter of personal choice; 'synthetic leather' has either a thin layer of textile material as backing or an additional intermediate layer of plastic foam. The former is for flat-surfaced base material, the latter for very uneven surfaces or where additional thermal insulation is needed (for solid-laminate or metal partitions).

The adhesive used is a special solvent-free glue, particularly suitable for work in poorly ventilated spaces.

You should never attempt to tackle large areas by yourself; at least two people are needed otherwise the adhesive covered sheet cannot be pressed precisely into position, and it is essential to get it in the right place first time.

1 The inside of the cabin superstructure is to be covered. First, take down the inside frames of the windows, then stick a strip of double-sided adhesive carpet tape along the upper edge of the window wall to hold the roughly cut sheet.

2 Using a sharp knife or scissors, cut out the holes for the windows. You will need a helper to press the sheet against the cabin wall to stop it sliding about.

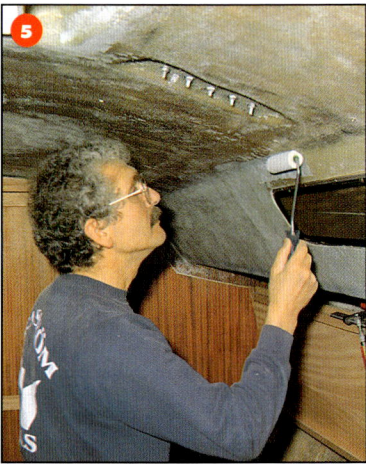

3 Using a cheap paintbrush, spread the glue evenly. The temperature when doing this should not be less than 15°C, otherwise the glue takes too long to set.

4 For large areas, you can use a paint roller as a spreader. Do check that the glue is spread evenly, especially right to the edges.

5 Next, the glue is applied to the cabin side wall. Adhesive fresh from the tin can be worked almost like thick paint; it doesn't become stringy.

6 Although initially the glue is almost white, after 10–20 minutes it becomes transparent. This is the stage when it starts to be adhesive and a start can be made fitting the sheet in place provided the glue on it has also become transparent.

7 Alignment marks, made when cutting the sheet to size, are a great help when fitting in place, since it can't really slide about. It is necessary to get it right first time – start at the top edge and smooth downwards.

8 When fitting the sheet in position, don't trap any air bubbles between it and the wall: push out any that appear at once, using the edge of the hand. Blobs of surplus glue must be removed immediately from the vinyl with solvent supplied by the manufacturer. You can use water to remove glue that is still moist.

9 Where the surface is contoured in a big way, the sheet will have to be held in place for the whole of the setting phase (overnight) by means of a small stay.

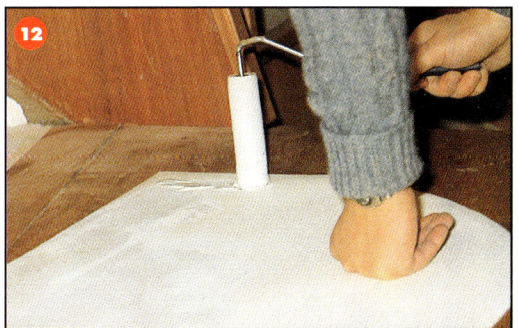

10 To 'beautify' the underside of the deck, first of all cut sheets of 6 millimetre marine plywood accurately to size.

11 The finished plywood panel is laid on the plastic sheet as a template; make sure it's on the right side. When cutting the sheet, allow about an extra 5 centimetres as a border all round.

12 Apply the glue to the sheet first, taking particular care that it is spread evenly around the edges; then leave it for 10–20 minutes.

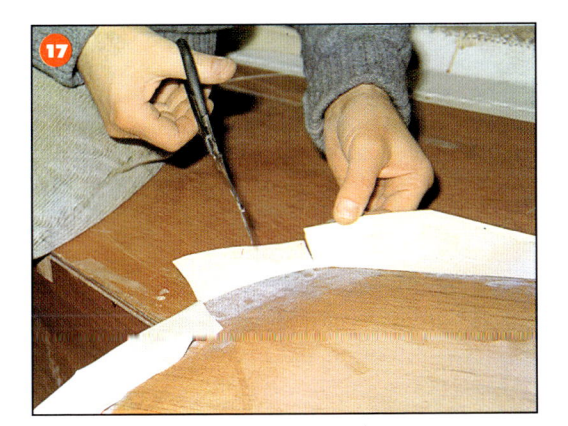

13 Then apply glue to the plywood panel. Glue dries more quickly on wood, so always apply the glue to this last.

14 Now lay the panel on the sheet and apply glue around the exposed side panel edges for the sheet border. Large parts should only be cut to size on the boat, the gluing being done in the workshop where there is more room.

15 Radiuses (curves) are cut to shape and glued to the back. If the glue isn't holding yet, use adhesive tape for a temporary fix.

16 The narrow strips are first pulled vertically upwards, then pressed down on to the back of the panel.

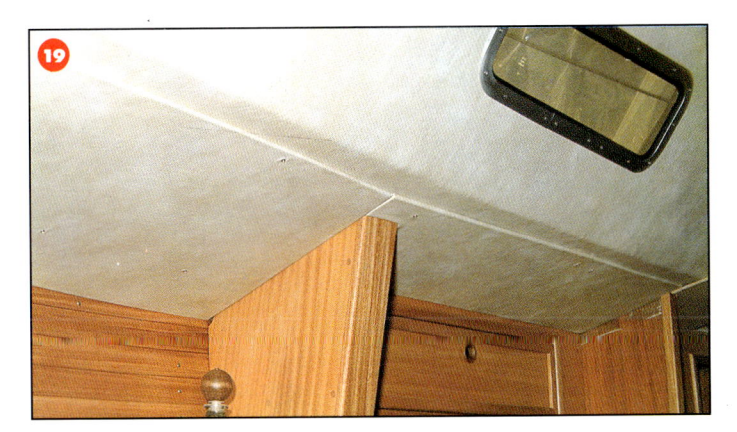

17 In the case of external radiuses, small wedges are cut out of the border to avoid any double thickness of material.

18 Fold the long edges over, one at a time, and press them down with the ball of the thumb, also ensuring that no air bubbles are trapped.

19 Here the finished headlining is fixed in place using self-tapping screws.

20 Lastly, a batten with a 'step' milled into the back is fitted to cover the edge. Any unevenness will not show up so much if this is done.

Making curves and corners

Round the corner we go: in this section we describe the 'rounding-off' technique which makes the difference between plain box construction and the work of the discriminating boatbuilder. Rounded corners are not only attractive; they are also kindly to body contact and make sense ergonomically.

The interior of a sailing yacht fitted out in wood is given character primarily by the presence of gentle curves and radiuses. Not only because of appearances: the great strength of such constructional characteristics and the reduced risk of injury are much more important. If, for instance, in a seaway you knock against a table corner that has been expertly rounded off, this should have no unpleasant consequences.

Generations of boatbuilders have kept such uncertainties in mind when doing fitting out work. What this means is that parts such as handrails, table edges, bunk corners, companionways and engine casings must always be finished with rounded corners/edges.

Through the trade you can obtain a wide range of profiled battens and semi-finished pieces of teak or mahogany. It is not advisable for a DIY builder to try and produce these himself because the dimensional precision which is particularly important here is practically impossible to achieve using tools readily available.

The tricky thing is the choice of colour. Teak

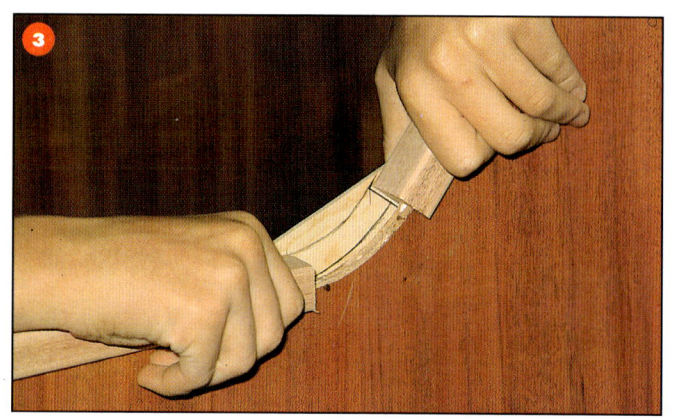

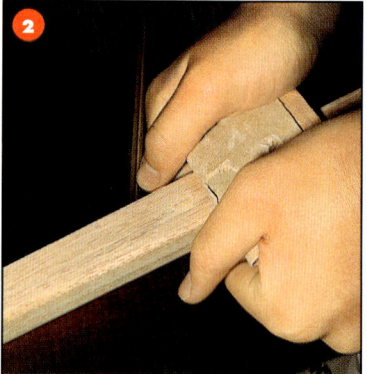

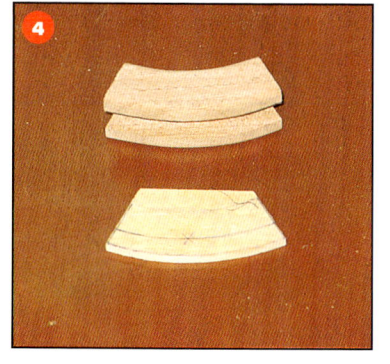

usually has only minor colour gradations so that matching is less of a problem. On the other hand, with mahogany, you should try to order all the profiled battens and strips you are going to need at the same time to ensure that they are all cut from the same trunk. This does mean more planning time, but you recover that easily later by taking less time for the job. Having decided on certain profile shapes you should endeavour, as far as possible, to use these throughout, to present a co-ordinated appearance. Mixing them has the further disadvantage that surfaces and joins don't fit together.

1 The sharp edge of a waist-high galley bulkhead is to have an edging strip. The profiled strip is 30 millimetres wide and 25 millimetres deep. The groove for the plywood panel needs to be 12 millimetres wide. When ordering this strip from the carpenter, it is a good idea to let him have a small sample of the plywood. Sheets do vary somewhat in thickness, so a sample is the only means of ensuring he mills the groove exactly right. Since these glued-on edgings are also load bearing, a tight fit is absolutely necessary. The strip is first cut to length, the end ground to an exact right angle on the angle grinder, glue applied, and then screwed on.

2 The first (horizontal) strip is screwed and plugged; the plug then rubbed down neatly.

3 The strip for the slanting length is also cut precisely to length but not yet screwed on since the angle piece has to be made first. With both strips fixed in position, hold a small offcut against the underside and transfer the measurements and contours on to a template with a very sharp pencil.

4 Using that template the carpenter can shape the closing piece. This is precision work, but with the right tools you can, of course, do it equally well yourself.

5 The shaped piece is inserted; the other strips pushed up against it.

6 Having done this, check that the ends butt neatly (if need be, grind some more, but don't round off the edges!).

7 The angle piece has glue applied, is screwed on and plugged. The joins with the strips are rubbed down level. Next the whole thing is primed with thinned down varnish (20:80); only then will you see how good the fit really is. After this priming, the fine rubbing down begins, and repeated varnishing with undiluted varnish.

8 Profiles are important: this photograph shows that you can obtain just about any shape you like. Some joinery firms have geared their work programme particularly towards yacht fitting out. These shapes can be obtained in most of the widely used kinds of wood.

9 Finished teak (sometimes mahogany) grab handles can be obtained from major boatfitters. These items usually come from the Far East so the measurements can't be changed.

10 A grab handle after final varnishing; the mitres and surfaces have been neatly finished.

11 This particularly successful treatment of a corner junction shows that a lot of work can be put into producing a 'well-rounded' appearance.

12 The exact opposite: the mitre has been cut at the wrong angle. The mitre joint line *must* bisect the angle so that the two cut edges are the same length. Here they are not, and cannot be brought together properly.

13 In between the round and the half-round bar there is the dovetail bar. This is a splendid shape for making corner connections.

14 Dovetail bar used on a bunk side-board, seen from above.

15 Fine glasspaper is used to smooth the surface from plywood panel to profiled strip. Here also the screw holes have been properly plugged.

16 Even edging for windows and portholes can be machine finished. Using such semi-finished parts can save you a lot of time and effort.

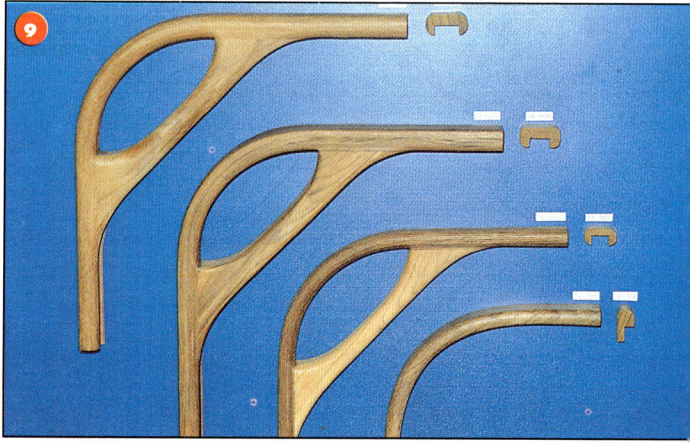

41

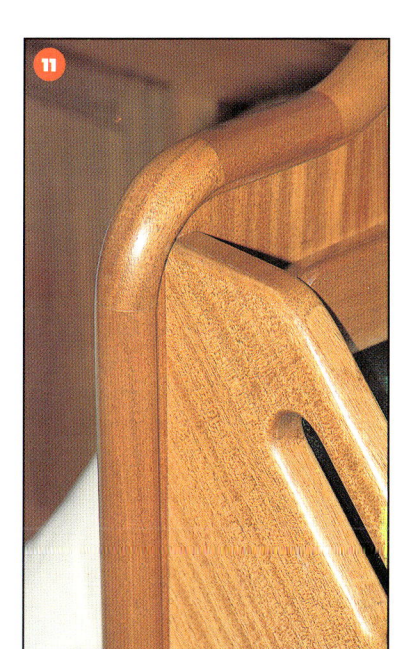

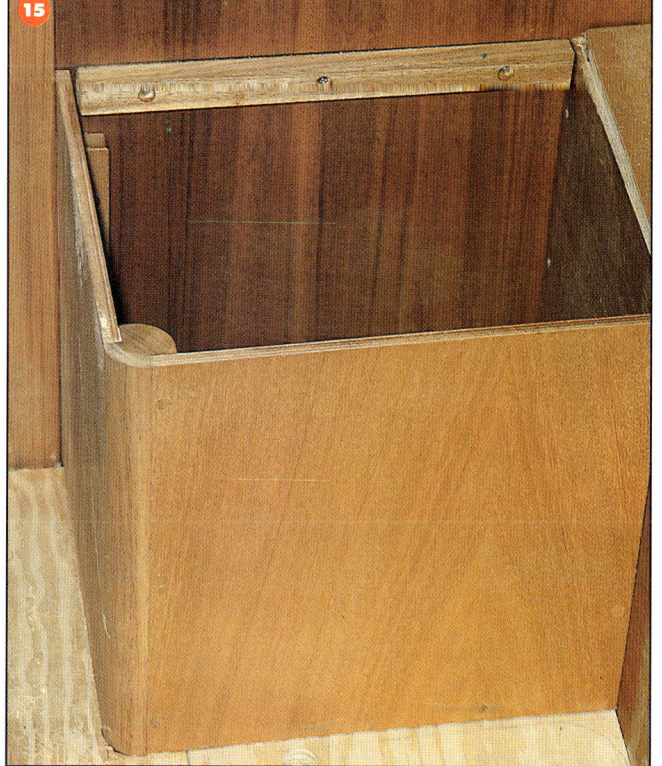

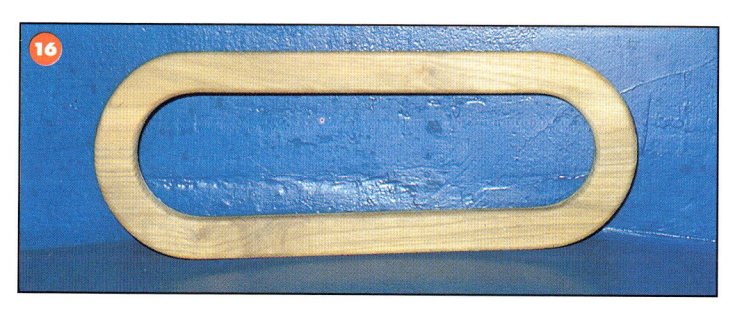

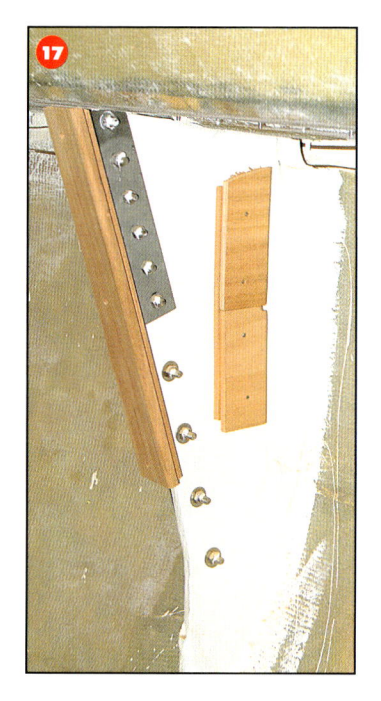

17 The chainplate is to be covered in. Here the corners of the shaped section strip that will be visible later on have also been rounded. This strip is screwed to the web frame. The plywood patches part way along the side will be used for fixing the finishing panels.

18 First of all, a template of thin, low quality plywood is made and fitted.

19 The precisely shaped side panel is screwed to the shaped strip at the front, and to the patches in the middle. To hold it more securely the contact surfaces are first coated with waterproof glue.

20 Before varnishing, the difference in colour between the surface of the plywood and the wood for the plugs was scarcely noticeable, but varnishing has highlighted it: the plugs are too dark.

Wood cladding for inner hull and headlinings

The headlining on the inside of a sailing yacht is primarily for decorative purposes. But thermal insulation, condensation, throughflow of air and soundproofing present problems which must not be overlooked at the planning stage.

The task of fitting a headlining is easiest where the yacht hull is of sandwich construction. There, the necessary layer of insulation – an intermediate layer of foam or balsawood – is already present and you can start straightaway to screw on the ceiling support battens. With a solid laminate hull, things are different; here you must first of all fit the battens forming the substructure. Best used for this are lengths of plywood, 6–8 millimetres thick (depending on the hull curvature). These strips, some 8 centimetres wide, are glued to the inside of the hull with epoxy adhesive, being pressed against it by battens cut to length, and braced against the opposite side of the hull. This pressure has to be applied very carefully, otherwise the contact between strips and hull will not be even.

At least two layers of plywood should be glued one on top of the other in this way so that there is at least a thickness of 12 millimetres to accommodate screws. The tip of the screw must never project through the plywood strip when screwed in, or it will push the strip away from the GRP surface. If the hull is metal, the battens for the substructure are bolted to previously welded on brackets or directly to the inner flanges of stringers and frames if they are present.

As already mentioned, the hull of a GRP sandwich yacht provides insulation against temperature differences and noise so that there is little danger of condensation forming.

Solid laminate and metal hulls must, however, have a layer of insulation inserted between hull and ceiling. Mineral wool panels and sprayed on rigid foam have proved useful for this purpose and there are a number of trade products available.

When fitting any headlining, it is important to avoid any possibility of condensation accumulating between the hull surface and the insulating layer, so there must be a direct bond between the two. The example shown here is a GRP sandwich construction with a balsawood core. The inside skin of GRP is about 4 millimetres thick, that is strong enough to hold screws. Before starting to do any screwing, check that the drill and screw diameter match precisely. As a rule, a 3 millimetres hole is right for a 3.5 millimetre stainless steel self-tapping Phillips screw.

1 The positions for substructure battens are marked with a felt pen. For appearances' sake, these markings should be precisely vertical, since later the row of screws here will also be vertical. The easiest way of getting the line right is with a short plumb line – a spirit level or a set square is of no use here.

2 First screw in the centre screw; the batten then follows the hull form easily; the screws holding the top and bottom come next.

3 For a bunk about 2 metres long, three vertical battens evenly spaced are enough.

4 Then the headlining battens are screwed on, working from the bottom upwards – for two reasons: firstly, the bunk edge indicates the horizontal line; secondly, it's easier to press a batten down from above against the one underneath. Since this work involves a continuous interchange between drill, countersink and screwdriver it is best if two people do it – one to hand the tools, the other to use them. Importantly, make sure you drill only through the *inner* layer of laminate; without care you can easily drill a hole in the outer skin.

5 The final battens under the deck are the most difficult, since firstly they taper and secondly have to be fitted, for example, around fittings, bolt ends, etc. Behind these last battens electric leads and hoses can also be easily hidden.

6 It is best to run the headlining continuously and build in the cupboards or shelves later.

7 A section of assembled and varnish-primed headlining in the after cabin: the next job is lining the deck underside.

8 This hanging cupboard has been built in after the headlining has been laid. To insert a headlining into one of these narrow cupboards retrospectively would be very difficult.

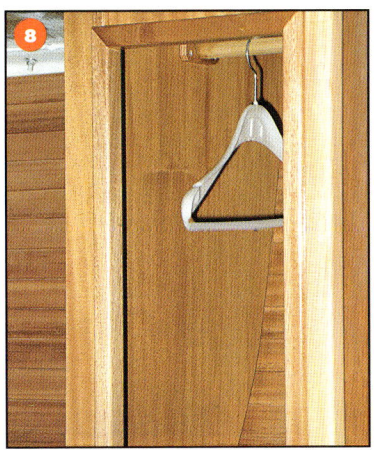

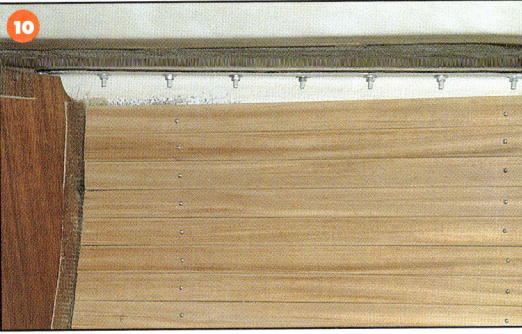

9 Short headlining strips in the saloon: first the horizontal is established using a spirit level, then the precise position is marked in.

10 The lengths have to be just right, because the end covering strips applied later only compensate for minor dimensional variations.

11 The finished headlining – graining and colour are correct. You will have to apply three or four coats of varnish to get a smooth finish. This is a more general view, to show how the headlining fits into the overall picture.

The fresh water system

To provide a minimum level of comfort in a sailing yacht you need a fresh water system with a tank, electric pump, accumulator and a tap in both the galley and the heads compartment. Here we show how this system is installed.

A pressurised water system on board can take many different forms – depending on the owner's requirements. The simplest and cheapest solution would be a flexible water bag in combination with a mechanical foot pump. For regular daily use this form of water supply however involves substantial inconvenience. For instance, water bags are quite fragile and sharp edges or projecting glass fibres can quickly cause a leak. Operation of a mechanical hand/foot pump doesn't exactly give a convenient result because you can't produce an evenly flowing jet. In short, this solution may suffice for day sailers, but it's no good for a sailing yacht which requires a degree of comfort.

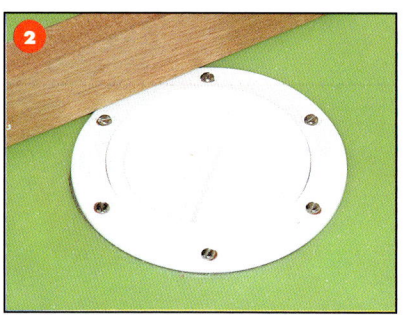

Rigid tanks, either of stainless steel (expensive), or of impact-resistant PVC, have proved a practical solution. In both cases it is important that there is a covered inspection hole in the top. If possible, the tanks should be installed amidships, because water adds weight to the boat – 100 litres weighs 100 kilograms.

Extra large tanks have not proved a success in practice, because from one weekend to the next the water isn't used up quickly enough and may become a health risk. If, however, you want to store a large volume of water, two medium-sized tanks are better than a large one. These can be connected separately to the system.

Electric pumps feed the system. When buying a pump, check that the pumping capacity is adequate and that it isn't noisy. There are some that cannot be used at night because the noise would wake the whole crew. Between pump and taps there should additionally be an accumulator which has two important duties: firstly it prevents the pump starting and stopping at short intervals even if no water has been drawn off, and secondly turning the taps on and off doesn't start/stop the pump so abruptly; that is, the accumulator acts as a form of shock absorber. When locating the filling connection on deck, pick somewhere a long way from the fuel filler to prevent mix-ups – that advice is based on experience, believe me!

1 Inspection hole flange piece and cover, filling connection fitting, tank and hull vent connection pieces. The vent pipe may lead directly outboard (roughly at deck level). In the case of yachts with a true bilge it is better to run the vent so that it has a gooseneck in it, and have it ending in the bilge. There will also be one less hole in the hull.

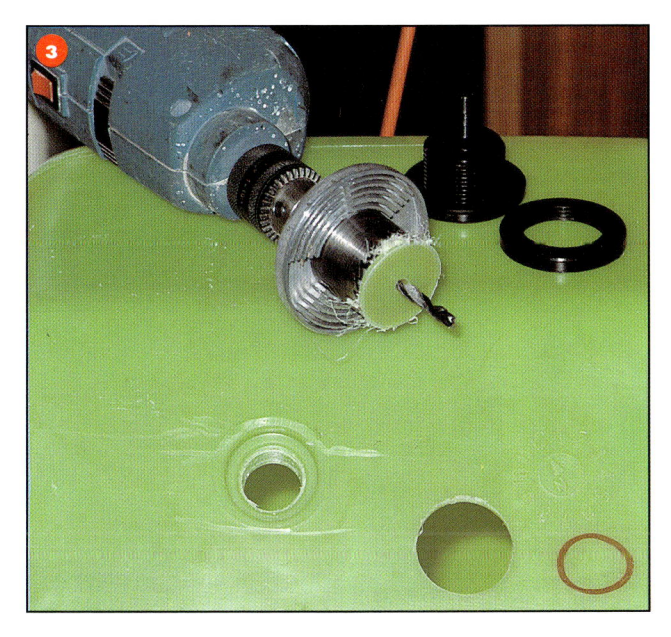

2 Using an electric jig saw, cut the inspection hole and fix the (white) flange piece with self-tapping screws. Either fit a separate gasket or use silicone sealant because water may press against the cover if the boat heels over.

3 The smaller holes are cut with a hole saw. Work with a low rate of advance, to avoid the PVC becoming hot and melting.

4 When you have fitted the connection pieces from inside the tank, via the inspection hole, you fasten on the fabric-reinforced hoses by means of stainless steel hoseclips. The connection piece pipe stud and hose bore must match precisely.

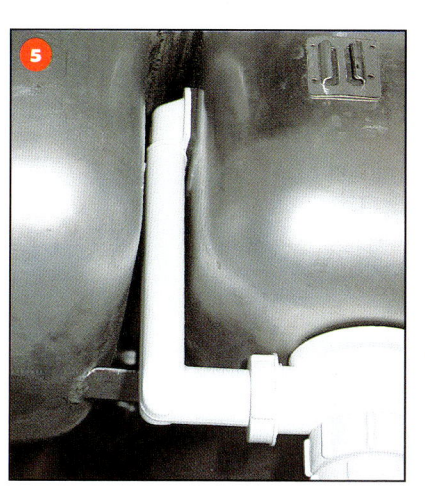

5 When buying a basin, check that it has an overflow opening, otherwise you're sure to have a flood at some stage.

6 Drains are brought together via PVC pipes which can be cut to length with a sharp handsaw. Apertures which will not have a hose or pipe connected are sealed with sheet gasket.

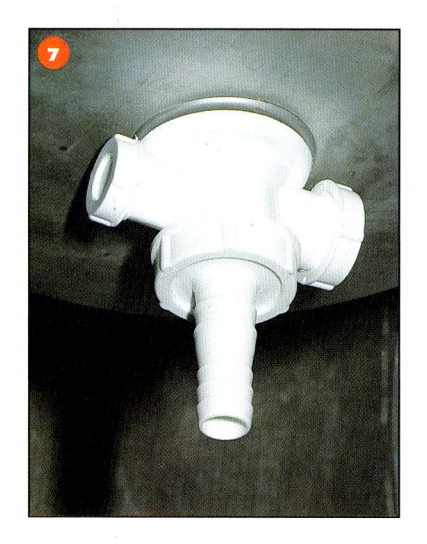

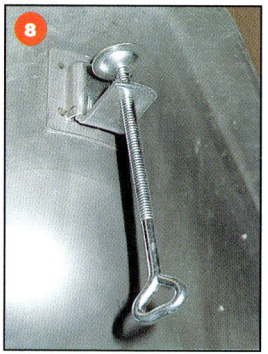

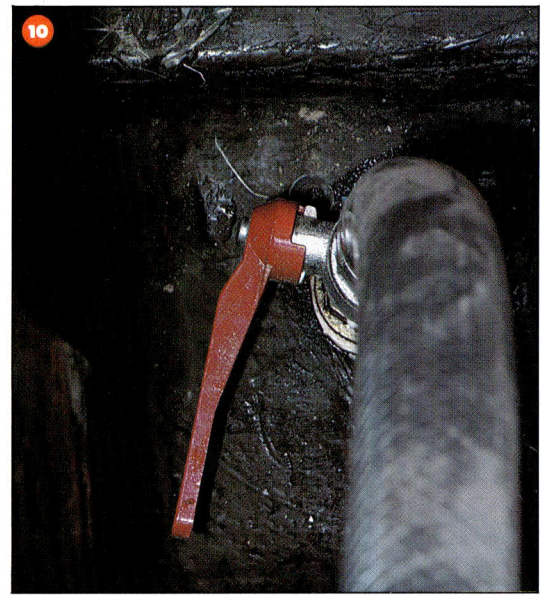

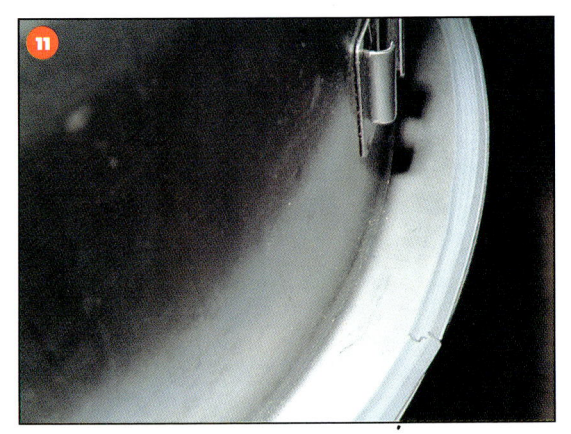

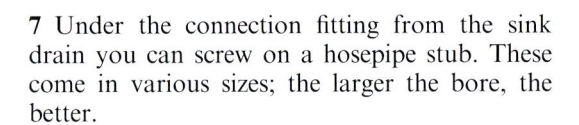

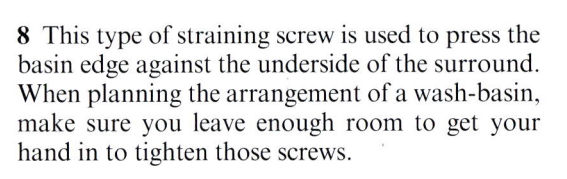

7 Under the connection fitting from the sink drain you can screw on a hosepipe stub. These come in various sizes; the larger the bore, the better.

8 This type of straining screw is used to press the basin edge against the underside of the surround. When planning the arrangement of a wash-basin, make sure you leave enough room to get your hand in to tighten those screws.

9 The tap from the builders' merchant: inexpensive, rugged and reliable. To connect it to the supply you just use a garden hose connection fitting.

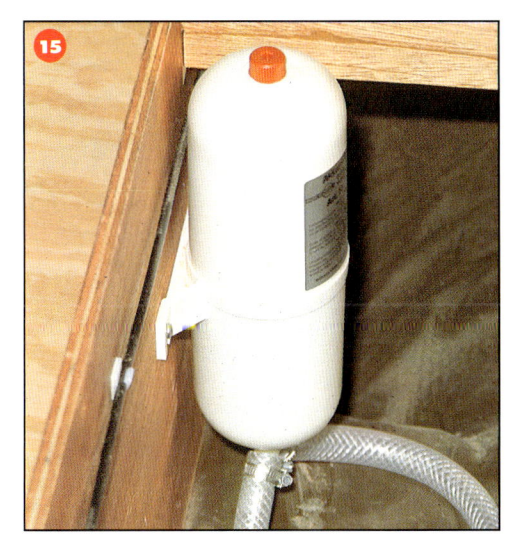

10 The sea cock for the drain must be easily accessible and should preferably be directly underneath the sink. Any bend in the hose slows down the draining process.

11 Before fitting the steel basin in position, a ring of foam rubber is glued underneath its edge. This prevents water penetrating between edge and table and also avoids damage to the surface varnish by the sharp edge.

12 The tap also has a rubber sealing ring underneath its mounting flange. This steadies it and substantially lengthens the life of the varnish around it.

13 All hoses below deck should be run with generous bends, and holes through GRP generously dimensioned and the edges rounded.

14 The equipment underneath a bunk. In sequence tank, pump and accumulator. Always run wiring for electricity at such a height that it is out of the way of any water that may leak from the fittings.

15 The accumulator is simply screwed to the bulkhead. Its inlet and outlet connections are at the bottom.

The water supply system

The diagram shows the arrangement of the individual components of the water supply system of a yacht.

To the right, the tank, in this example made from PVC. You may of course prefer stainless steel, but that would be substantially more expensive. I don't consider so-called hosepipe tanks, that is soft ones, really suitable for long-term use in yachts. The tank has a filling pipe and a vent pipe, ending above deck. The run of both is planned so that they will later be concealed inside cupboards. The vent pipe usually ends in a small terminal fitting penetrating the hull at rubbing strake level. If you don't want that sort of arrangement, you can curve the pipe down into the bilge and into which excess water can run if overfilling occurs. You should always pick a tank with a covered inspection opening in the top, so that it can be cleaned from time to time.

The draw-off pipe is connected to the bottom of the tank and goes directly to the electric pump. From there, it goes on to the accumulator and finally to the individual taps. It does not matter how many there are, it's just a question of inserting the appropriate number of branch fittings.

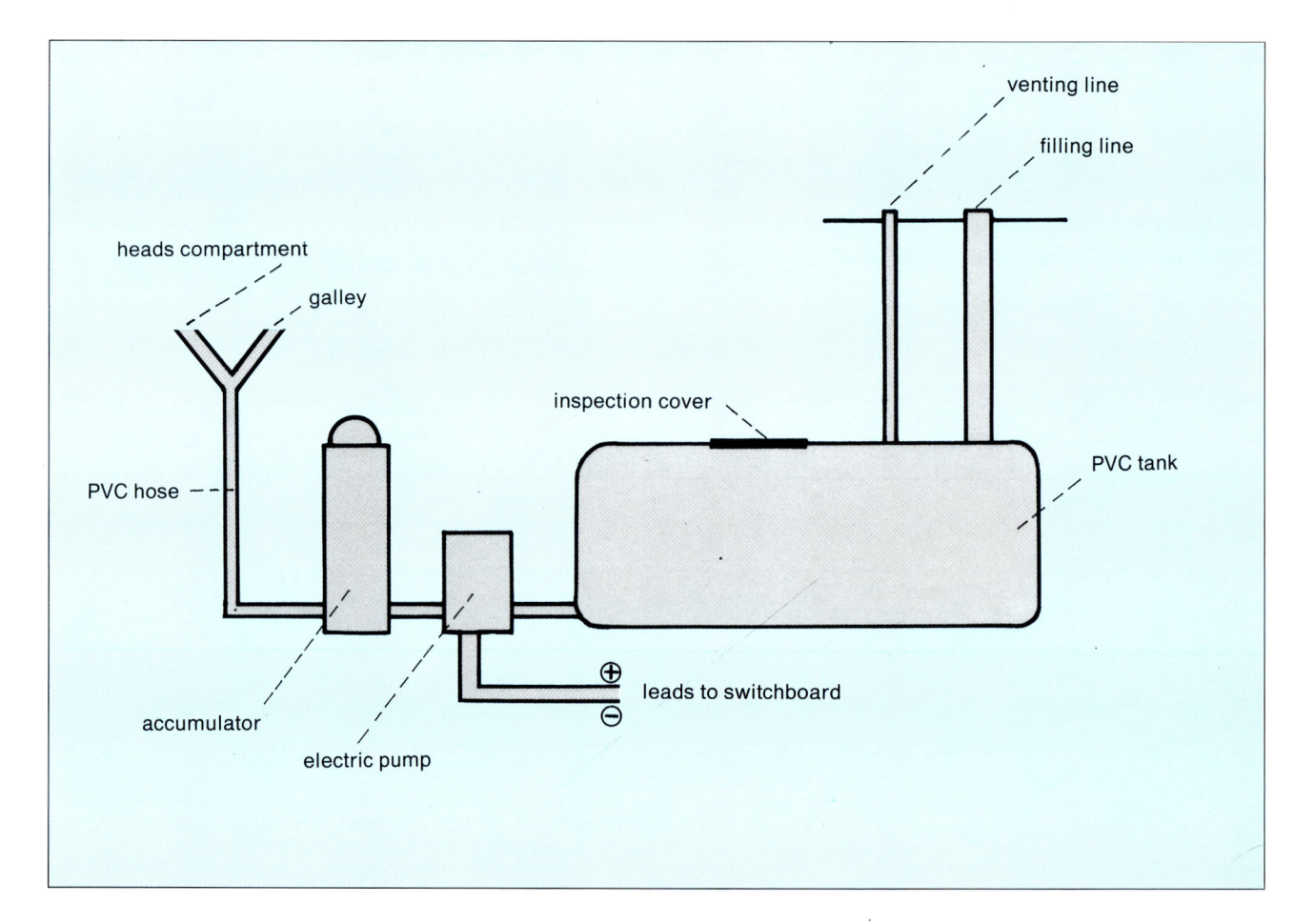

Chart table and locker

The heart of a sailing yacht is, and will continue to be, the navigator's corner. This is where all the strands of the power supply come together, and where the course to steer is determined. Careful planning of this area is therefore a *must*.

1 You start with the supporting bar for the table, which is fixed (glued and screwed) to the bulkhead precisely horizontally. You must work with great precision when setting this up, because all subsequent dimensioning is based on this bar. The best height for the table is about 70 centimetres.

2 The table baseplate is fastened to this bar, and the profiled bar to form the corner cut to length and the front panel cut ready.

3 Front panel, corner piece and side panel are glued and screwed to the baseplate.

Even if, due to modern electronics, navigation is progressively becoming simpler and more precise – I wouldn't like to do without a chart table and a proper navigator's locker. After all, the navigator's corner isn't just a chart table; here all electricity supply cables, aerials and control lines come together. Here, instruments for navigation, radio telephone equipment, weather instruments and distribution boards have to be accommodated.

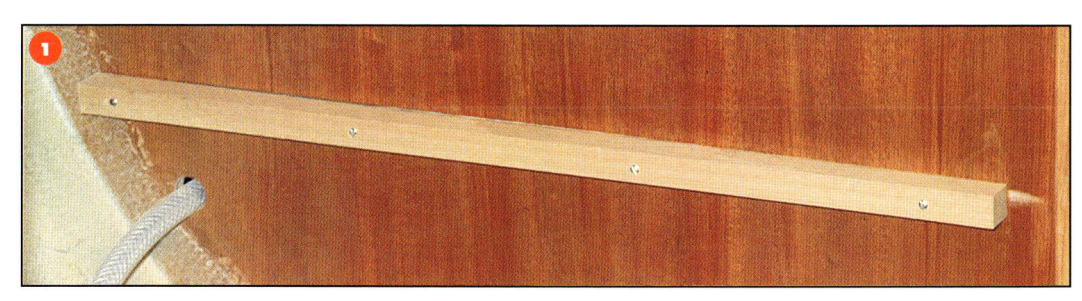

Before starting any work on board, every owner should compile a list of all necessary equipment. Every item then has its space requirement marked on a drawing (manufacturers' literature give the exact dimensions). You also have to decide on the number of fused circuits. A board with six sets of switches and fuses is the absolute minimum. For a 10 metre yacht, 12 circuits are really the norm, and even then some fuses have to serve several outlets. The principle I recommend here is, to be generous in planning your capacity because, over the years, you're bound to want to add new navigation equipment.

The size of the table depends on the charts you intend to use. For recreational cruising charts, a 70 × 50 centimetre table is about right. That also provides a large enough area for a 'merchant navy' chart quartered. If there is adequate room, 100 × 80 centimetres is the size to aim for.

4 The screw holes are plugged and the plugs rubbed down. The corner piece is also rubbed down and the edges rounded off with glasspaper.

5 The side portion of the table top is glued on and has an edging strip fitted. The strip is mitred at the corner.

6 The strip to complete the corner is also glued and screwed on, with screws about 35 millimetres long. Since you don't expect to get humidity here, you can use screws that are either galvanised or cadmium-plated.

7 When finish-grinding the corner, first of all just mark the curvature and cut back to that. Don't smooth and round off the edges until the next stage.

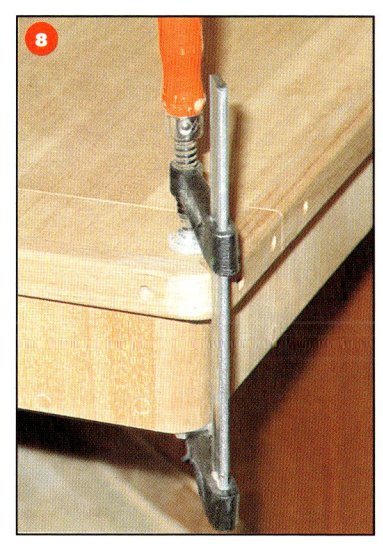

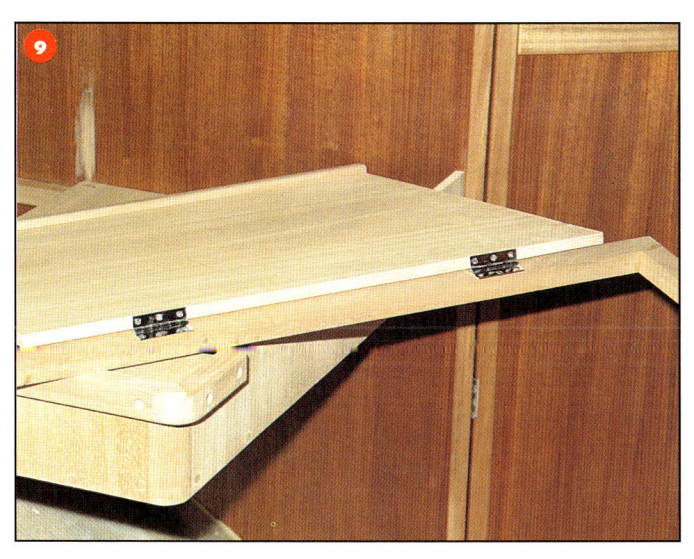

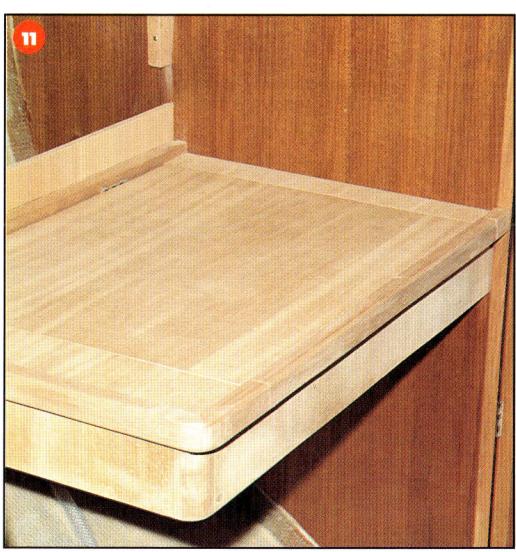

8 When putting together the table top flap, check that the gap between the fixed and moving part is parallel – it should be about 1 millimetre wide to allow for the coats of varnish.

9 The hinges are screwed to the frame which subsequently is glued to the panel closing the back of the chart stowage. This makes fitting the hinges much easier than after installation.

10 The frame is glued and screwed to the bulkhead. Check that the flap is an exact fit at the front and the side, because adjustment later is not possible.

11 A strip of plywood closes off the chart stowage at the back. The front panel of the navigator's locker is later fixed to this strip.

12 Before installing this panel, the bookshelf and partition have to go in. You will find it difficult to get at these later, so they should already have been primed, rubbed down and varnished.

13 The front panel of the instrument locker is initially only cut roughly to shape and fitted. The strips remaining alongside the cut out apertures should all be about the same width.

14 The front panel for the locker under the table is made in the same way, and has to be set back far enough to leave room for the knees.

15 The insert panel, which will accommodate the instruments, has a reinforcing bar and a piano hinge fitted along its bottom edge.

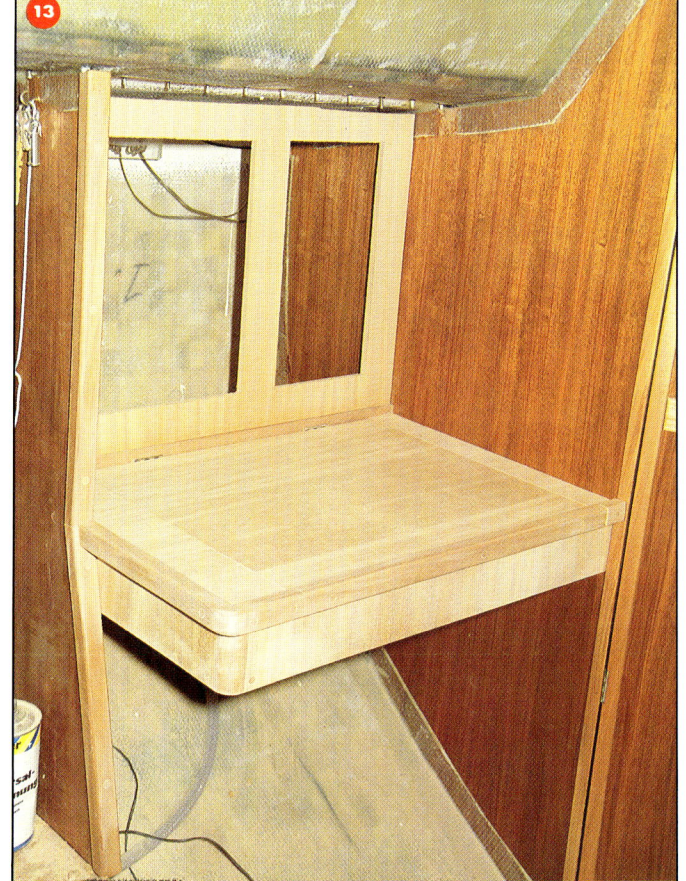

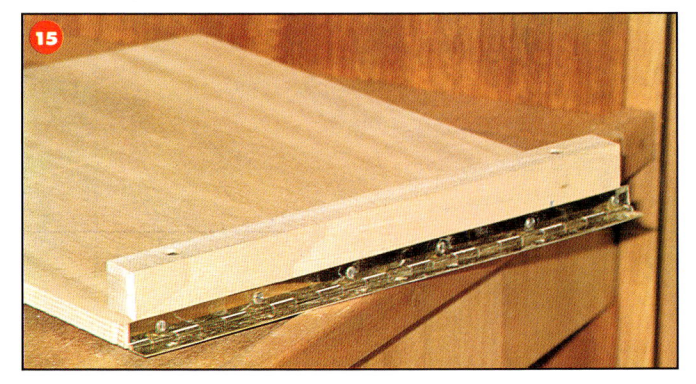

16 At the top, a proper lock is screwed to the inside. Here, a lock is preferable to a catch, because the instruments to be fitted are quite heavy.

17 Before screwing the panel hinge to the frame, the apertures for the instruments should be cut out and the fit checked roughly.

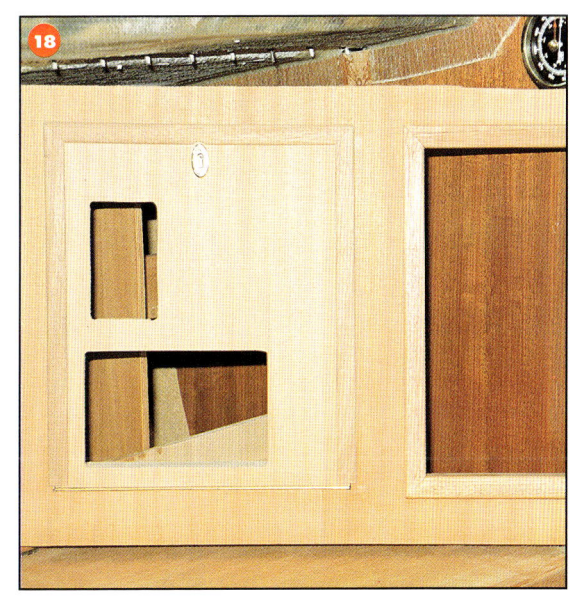

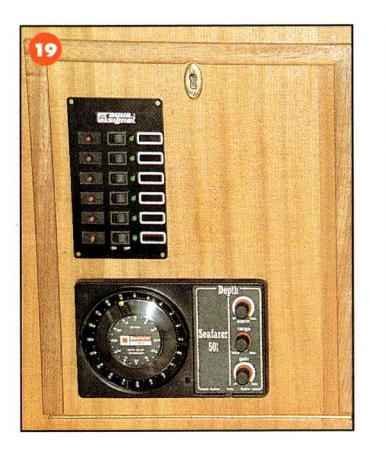

18 The carpentry is now completed and the front can be fitted to the frame. Before final installation of the panel, it is advisable to prime it with diluted varnish and rub it down.

19 When varnishing has been completed, a start can be made with the final installation of the instruments. The piano hinge gives easy access to the back of the instruments.

20 The negative lead is connected to a bridge before it is wired to the distribution board. The positive leads are connected directly to the switch via a plug and socket.

21 The navigator's corner is almost complete. It's not essential for the bottom locker to have a door since you can only see into and use the lower part.

22 If navigation equipment is due to take up all the space above the table, a car radio and cassette player can also be installed underneath it.

23 The front of the radio must not stick out, rather it must be set back from the table edge, otherwise it's too easy to knock off the operating knobs.

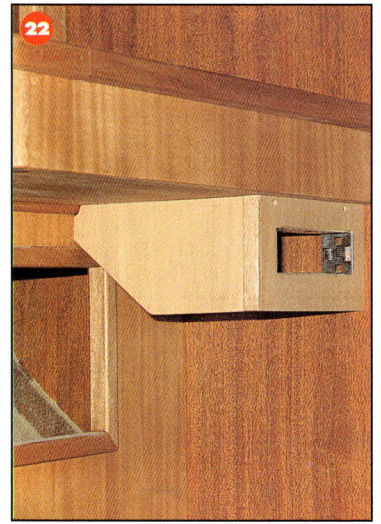

Fitting out the galley

Anyone who stints on space and expense for the galley of a cruising yacht will surely regret it later. Working surfaces, equipment and stowage spaces have to be scaled to match the number of crew normally on board.

Racing sailors won't bother to give a lot of thought to the layout of a galley; they're satisfied with a small water tap and drain and a simple cooker. But the cook who has to feed a crew of four or more has to operate at this 'work station' up to three times a day; if he (or she) has to put up with deficiencies all the time, cooking becomes a penance.

The minimum for a 10 metre yacht is the following: double bowl sink, gas cooker with oven, water under pressure and a swivel tap, a refrigerator or icebox and, of course, ample stowage space based primarily on crew numbers. When I did my planning, I did not always apply the normal standards but rather went my own way and later found this to be right. For example, my galley working surface is much higher than usual, with the advantages that, firstly, you can work standing upright and needn't bend over the sink, and secondly, there is room under the double bowl sink for a commercial refrigerator. The standard height for galley working surfaces is about 85 centimetres – I took it up to 1 metre. This permitted fitting a refrigerator with a door which is of course far more practical than a cold chest accessible from above (that always has something lying on the lid!). Additionally, an upright refrigerator is easier to keep tidy than a chest. The disadvantage of the former is that every time it is opened a little 'coolness' is lost, but in practice it is insignificant.

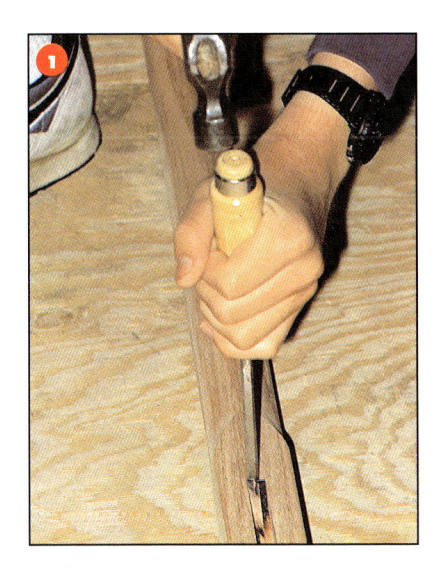

1 The galley corner post: it's not only something for the crew to grab hold of but also steadies the midship end of the bulkhead. The groove in the post, initially machine milled, is lengthened at the top as necessary with a chisel.

2 The post must be set dead upright in both directions – fore and aft and athwartships. There is no possibility of correcting mistakes later; any made here would always show up.

When designing the cooker surround, once again I didn't use the standard approach, because almost all series production craft have the cooker installed so that it can indeed swing freely with the heel, but keeping the back parts clean is almost impossible. Should anything drop down between cooker and locker, retrieving it is usually a difficult job. So my principle was to leave plenty of space around the cooker, even if it meant a little less for storage. Even where stowage space in a galley is limited, with common sense and a bit of thought, room will be found for all the essentials.

The crockery and cutlery stowage above the cooker should have suitable holders and racks fitted right from the start. First buy the crockery, then construct the holders so that everything fits tightly and stays put even in a seaway. The sliding doors for the most important of the upper stowages were made of Perspex, letting more light into the cupboard and making it easier to find the right jar/tin. Before the sink and fittings are installed the working surface has to be varnished and in view of the heavy wear and tear it should have five or six coats (rubbed down between each).

3 Next, the little plywood frame is screwed to the sandwich deck underside with four (about 4 millimetre diameter) screws. But don't glue yet, because the post is going to have to be taken down once more before being permanently secured. Only then do you glue it in place and plug the screw holes.

4 The side, top and front panels have holes cut in them as necessary and are screwed and glued together. All right angles must be precise.

5 Piano hinges are laid on a flat surface for screwing on. That way you get the hinge in the right position relative to the front edge.

6 The almost finished, primed door is screwed to the frame – a bit of a tricky job. You will need a short screwdriver here.

7 Installing the refrigerator is relatively simple: the dark metal flange is screwed to the front panel. If this wooden panel is large, it should be reinforced on the inside with square battens to stop it buckling.

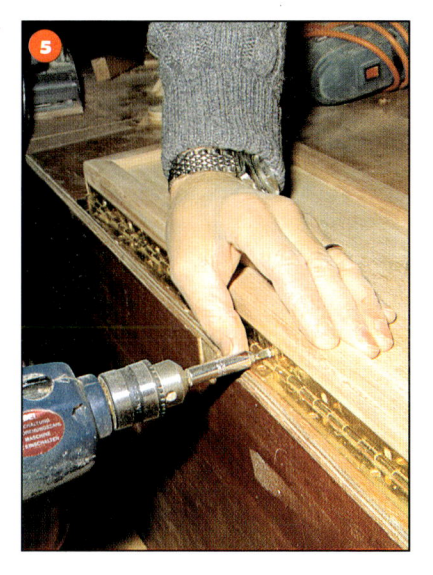

8 The edging strip along the back of the working surface is drilled all along its length to allow hot air from the refrigerator to escape. The large hole (left) is for the water tap.

9 I didn't screw the cooker mounting bracket directly to the bulkhead but on to a post, creating a space between cooker and bulkhead.

10 This drilled ledge stops the cooker moving freely if the boat heels. A bolt with a grippable head can replace the temporary one shown.

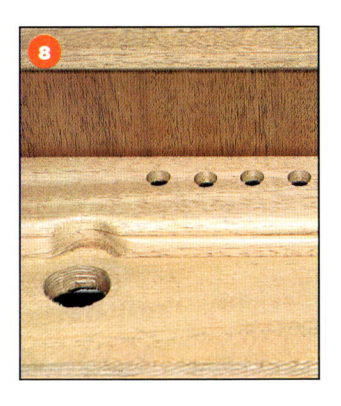

59

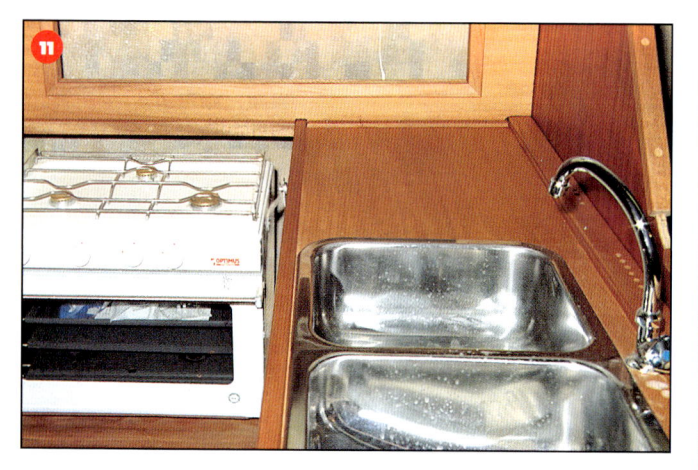

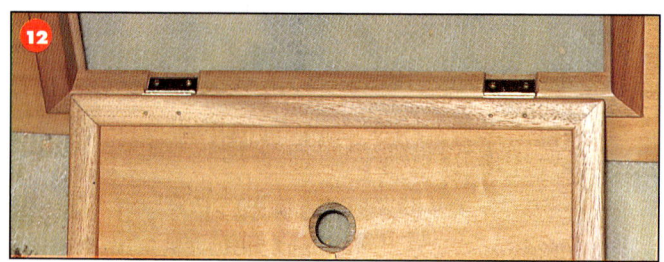

11 The cooker burners should be at about the same height as the galley working surface. This is particularly important if the cooker has been installed with only a small clearance around it (risk of burns).

12 Instead of the piano hinge, you could use two separate hinges for the lid of the lower stowage. Fitting is more difficult because you have to cut back the frame strip.

13 It needs only the ultraviolet radiation of a single sailing season for the various frame strips, which here differ substantially in colour, to acquire much the same shade.

14 Adequate illumination for this work place is important. Modern fluorescent lamps need only about 7 watts to give the same brightness as a conventional 25 watt bulb.

15 The Perspex sliding doors can be ordered made-to-measure from the trade, or you can cut them yourself using a jig saw. The finger hole has to be cut very carefully – on a smooth surface with a low rate of advance and low revs. Smooth the cut edges with glasspaper.

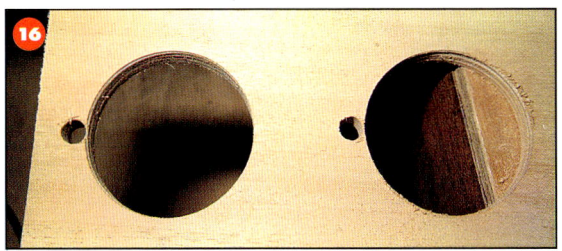

16 A mug holder, part-finished: with a cup-shaped cutter you make the large hole; alongside, the small one for the handle. The web between the holes is removed with a small saw.

17 Base and upper portion are joined (screws and glue) by means of a rectangular bar. The edges are then rounded and the holder varnished.

18 The first arrangement: plates below, mugs above. This is OK, but it wastes space.

61

19 Since the mugs are used a lot, I decided to mount the holder on the bulkhead above the working surface.

20 A long, continuous shelf makes better use of the space (for glasses and boxes/pots/tins). Bottom left: the cutlery compartments. It's an easy job to face the back with cork sheet. Several coats of clear varnish make the back wall easy to wipe down.

21 The finished galley: the refrigerator door has had a sheet of plywood (3 millimetre thick) glued to it to maintain overall colour harmony. The sides of the galley fittings have been given three coats of varnish, and five coats for the working surfaces.

The finished galley: the central feature is the three-burner cooker with a small oven. Contrary to what the yard proposed, I haven't hemmed it in closely but rather left plenty of room on both sides. In my opinion that is the only sensible arrangement for keeping the place clean – even if it does reduce potential storage space.

The locker for pots and pans is underneath the cooker; plates, cups, cutlery and spices are stowed on the shelf above it. The transparent doors give you a good view inside. (Sliding doors made of wood always block at least half the view.) The galley working surface is positioned high enough to allow a refrigerator to be fitted under the sink. Furthermore, working at this height (100 to 105 centimetres) is much more pleasant since you don't have to bend down. Solid grab handles provide a secure hold when needed. The space for the rubbish bin is alongside the refrigerator and the same door gives access to the sea valve.

The flooring is of prefabricated strip-plywood, which has been given four coats of varnish after laying.

The saloon: lockers, bunks and table

In the saloon, two requirements have priority: cosiness and convenience. Here you should still feel comfortable even when weather-bound in port. 'Warm' wood, matching colours and generous radiuses create the right atmosphere.

Wood in the saloon is not there only for appearances' sake. Wood also helps noise reduction and diffraction, provides useful thermal insulation and contributes to an agreeable 'climate' in the compartment. Wood is capable of absorbing moisture from the air – particularly important during the cold season. It is rare to find condensation in yachts fitted out in wood; plastics are distinctly inferior in this respect.

My design of the saloon had two main objectives. Firstly the floor space was to have minimal obstructions and secondly, the bunk seats were to be as comfortable as possible. The backrests were, therefore, to be at much more of an angle than is usual for craft of this size. Angling the backrests makes more headroom around the sides of the cabin necessary, so locker depth is reduced. I consciously accepted this relatively minor disadvantage, since a depth of about 40 centimetres still left plenty of stowage space.

In practice, it's worth experimenting with the exact angle of the backrests, because it also depends on seat height. The bunk is easily mocked up with a couple of pieces of foam. With regard to the plane of the seat, an angle of about 110 degrees should be about right.

When designing the table, table and seat height must be in the right proportions. When sitting upright the lower part of the arms should rest on the table, parallel to the surface. Then, it is useful if the table edge is directly above the bunk edge, and with the side flaps folded down should not be right in the middle of the gangway but rather over to one side. This leaves a passage free to the forward compartment and people can still go through, even when the bunk seats are occupied.

1 First the cupboard and other false floors are fitted, glued and screwed down. Care must be taken to shape the back edges to match that of the hull exactly, otherwise anything small which disappears down here will be lost forever.

2 Before starting work on the front panels, the backs have to be lined; later, it would be very difficult to get in there to do this. You should also run the electric wiring before starting to build cupboards.

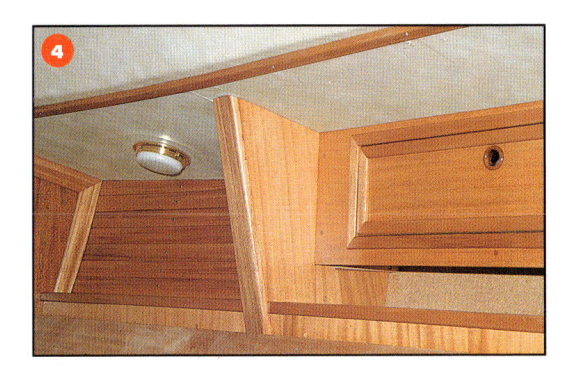

3 The locker is half finished. The toerail bolts have been left uncovered in case you have to get at them to deal with leaks. The deck underside is finally rubbed down and painted.

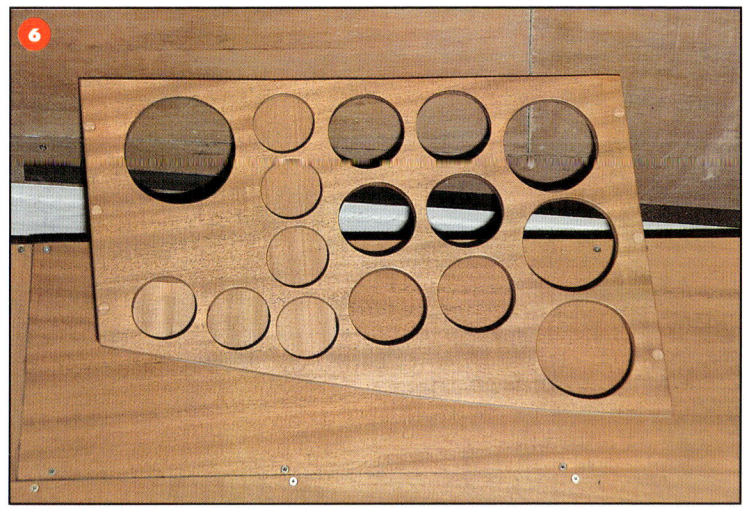

4 The finished frontage with two open shelves below and a closed locker above. Above the backrest, the edge is finished with a stout bar which serves as a handrail and provides support when the boat is heeling.

5 Since the backrests have to be foldable (to be raised for people to sleep in the bunks), extra-sturdy stainless steel hinges are screwed on left and right using M6 bolts.

6 A glass and bottle holder insert for the open shelf. This is just laid in from above, so that it is easy to take out for cleaning.

7 The bunk side panel is 12 millimetre plywood. The wooden corners are made with posts and dovetail joints to connect the panels.

8 Making a start with the saloon table. The support should be in the form of a slim central pillar so as to interfere as little as possible with leg room under the table.

9 Here profiled bars with an external radius are used. First you make two identical corner pieces, each comprising one front and one side panel. When completed these are screwed together to form the hollow pillar.

10 The table support half-finished. The pillar is subsequently screwed directly to the sole plate; that in turn is screwed to the bottom frames to mount the table very securely.

11 Once the table top has been cut to size, you start fitting the edging strips. These also have a radius to give the desired overall uniform appearance. The mitred corners are especially difficult to produce here since the table side flaps are trapezoidal; you don't get right angles at the corners. So the strip is first cut roughly to size, leaving spare.

12 That's the gap you get when you have cut the angle to 45 degrees. To get it right, you use the truing grinder.

13 An accurately mitred joint. You really can't do the precision grinding without a machine; when doing it by hand it's easy to inadvertently slightly round the mating surfaces.

14 Now that the edging strips fit precisely, they are pressed against the table top using screw cramps until the glue has set (at 20°C it takes about six hours).

15 Two piano hinges join up the three parts of the table. To screw these on, the table top parts are laid on a flat surface and accurately lined up. A helper should hold the parts firmly in position while the first screws are screwed in.

16 These stops (you will need two of them) are for holding the table flap supports in position. They are made from a 25 × 25 millimetre mahogany structural bar.

17 The table flap supports 'in action'. They are fastened to the central pillar, also using piano hinges. If you expect to heavily load the table it may be sensible to fit four supports.

18 When rubbing down and varnishing the table (the pillar with four, the top with at least five coats) has been completed, the fittings that prevent the flaps swinging in a seaway can be screwed on.

19 The smoothed and varnished edging strips fit very well and look good. I consider fiddles superfluous, since when the boat is heeling you don't normally eat at the table. But if you do want them, you should make them removable – they only get in the way when things are normal.

20 The completed saloon. The edges of the tables are directly above those of the bunk. The bunk backrests are more inclined than usual, which makes sitting more comfortable. Looking at the floor it can be clearly seen that the table is not central, in order to leave a passage as wide as possible when the flaps are down. If you prefer, you can make the pillar into a bottle rack.

A plan view of the table: the middle part is rectangular, the two flaps each have one side inclined to line up with the edge of the bunk.

Parts list:
Profile B battens	4 of	70 cm
Profile A battens	4 of	100 cm
Plywood 12 mm	2 of	70 × 26 cm
Plywood 12 mm	2 of	70 × 13 cm
Plywood 12 mm	1 of	77 × 25 cm
Plywood 12 mm	1 of	77 × 38 × 31.5 cm
Plywood 12 mm	1 of	77 × 29 × 24.0 cm

The folding-flap supports are cut from 20 × 20 centimetre plywood offcuts.

The external dimensions of the pillar are 19.5 × 32.5 centimetres, and the constituent plywood boards are respectively 13 and 26 centimetres wide.

Table height depends on bunk height and 70 centimetres would be normal. If the seats are relatively low, the table has also to be lowered otherwise it is not possible to sit comfortably. If the proportions are right, the table edge is just level with your elbows when you are sitting upright.

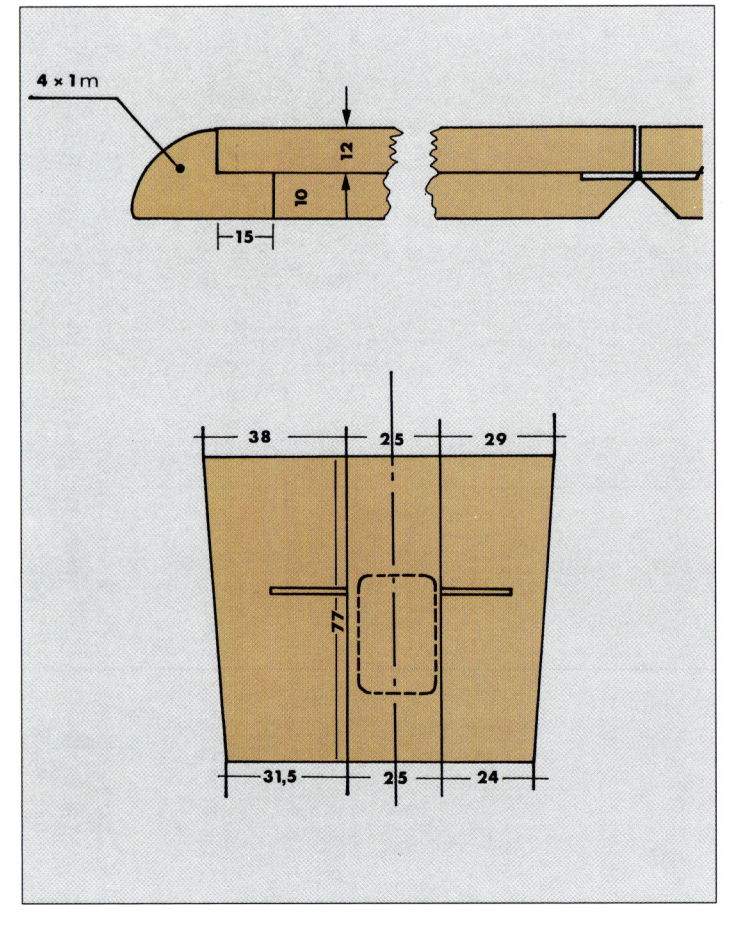

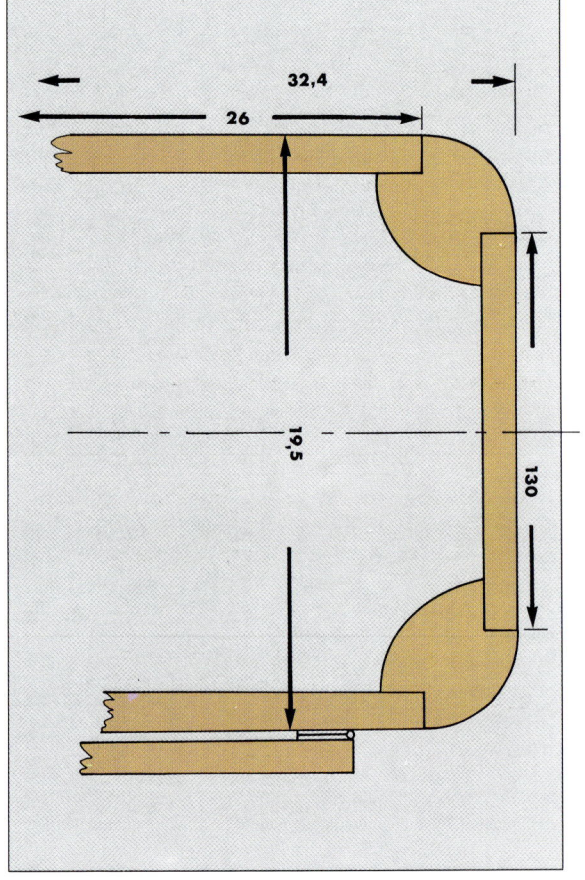

Fitting out the heads

Sanitation facilities are unfortunately a feature all too often neglected by cruising yacht designers; successful design depends on careful use of space and choice of equipment.

How often one finds that a good interior boat layout is marred by heads that are so cramped that even the most basic manoeuvre is difficult.

The heads compartment equipment and fittings of a cruising yacht should provide for every requirement of personal hygiene. It is even better if, space permitting, a shower is included in the plan.

In the example dealt with here – on board the CB-33 – a shower cubicle could be accommodated only with great difficulty, so it is all the more important to provide a really conveniently usable wash-basin over which you can comfortably bend. Furthermore, the surface to left and right of the large round basin are not just for show but are functional. Additional facilities provided include generous cupboard and stowage space for every member of the crew.

The seawater-flushed toilet must be rigidly mounted, comfortable to use and easy to clean. The sea cocks should be easy to find and easy to operate. The compartment itself should be easy to keep clean. Inaccessible nooks and crannies should be avoided as far as possible. There must be direct drainage to the bilge from under the heads floor so that, from time to time, a bucket of water can be poured into the area to flush it through thoroughly. Therefore all materials used here must be absolutely water/rustproof, and varnishing must be undertaken particularly carefully.

A ventilation system comprising two units is a good thing. There should be one permanently open vent (mushroom ventilator or similar) which is effective even when there is no one on board, and an easy-to-open hatch or window for light and air. The door to the saloon should obviously be made sound- and odour-proof as far as is possible.

Top quality lighting is equally important, because early morning and late evening are peak times for the compartment. There should be at least two 10 watt lamps, or economical fluorescent lights (7–10 watts) should be fitted.

1 First stage of work: the table top is fastened to the bulkheads at both ends by means of mounting bars. The cut out for the wash-basin is marked out with compasses, then cut with the jig saw.

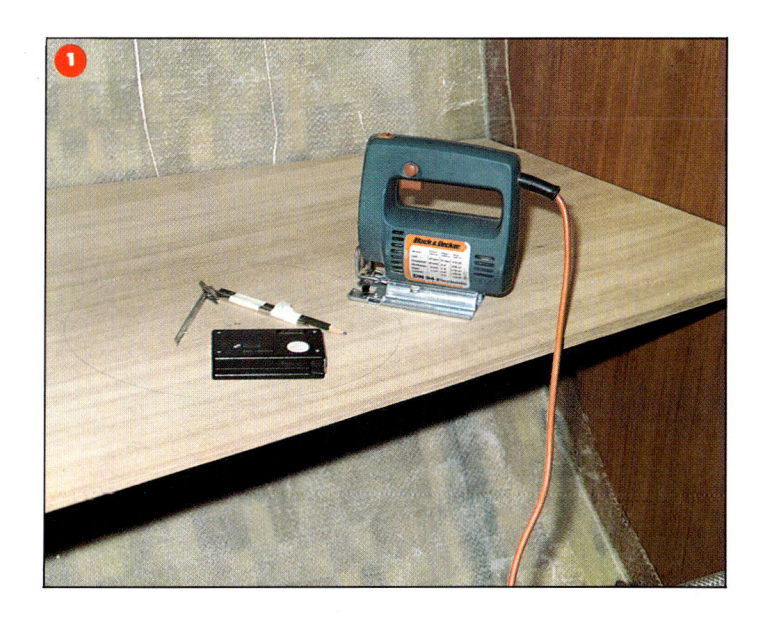

2 After installing the sink surround and the front panel below it, you fit the top cupboard front panel. The apertures have pre-machined (double grooved) edging strips fitted. The insert for the bottom cupboard is made and assembled outside it and installed, fully varnished, in one piece.

3 The wash-basin is fitted to check whether the supply and drainage hoses can be accommodated properly. Never lay the hoses as shown here (water flow is restricted); always look for the most direct run.

4 Sub-dividing the broken surface overhead is an awkward job. It is to be covered partly with glued on sheet vinyl, partly with coated plywood panels. Use a felt pen to mark out suitable areas for separate treatment.

5 Before the internal lining is glued in, the inside frame of this porthole must be removed. Don't replace the outside frame until you have finished applying glue.

6 The lining has now been applied and the inside frame has been screwed back on again. Take care to screw in all the screws a little at first, then screw down hard on opposite screws in turn.

7 The mounting for the light (the narrow panel overhead) is fitted in. It is also used to conceal the necessary wiring. The front edge of the panel is finished with a narrow edging strip to hide the plywood layering.

8 The lamp base is pre-fitted and the wiring is taken through to the back via a hole drilled to 10 millimetres diameter.

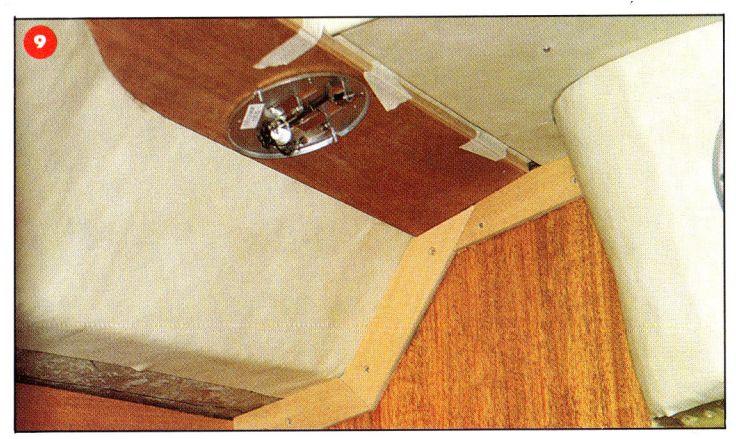

9 The panel with the lamp base is screwed in position. It is best to varnish this first and thus avoid the need for masking.

73

10 When you have finished varnishing the wooden parts, the shade and surround of the lamp can be fitted. The switch faces inboard to make it easier to find in the dark.

11 The two floor panels around the toilet are fitted. The back panel is screwed down securely as the pan will stand on it; the front panel is left loose on the bars for ease of cleaning underneath. There must be direct access to the bilge.

12 The pan is bolted to the floor plate with four M6 stainless steel bolts. Seat height can be adjusted by means of liners under the base. When planning the installation, check that you have left enough room for cleaning. The cork flooring adjoining the boards is set in epoxy adhesive and then given two coats of clear varnish.

13 Behind the heads compartment there is an oilskin locker, also with direct drainage to the bilge. A heating system outlet turns this into a drying cupboard. A sewage tank with a simple gravity drainage system will be fitted below the side deck later.

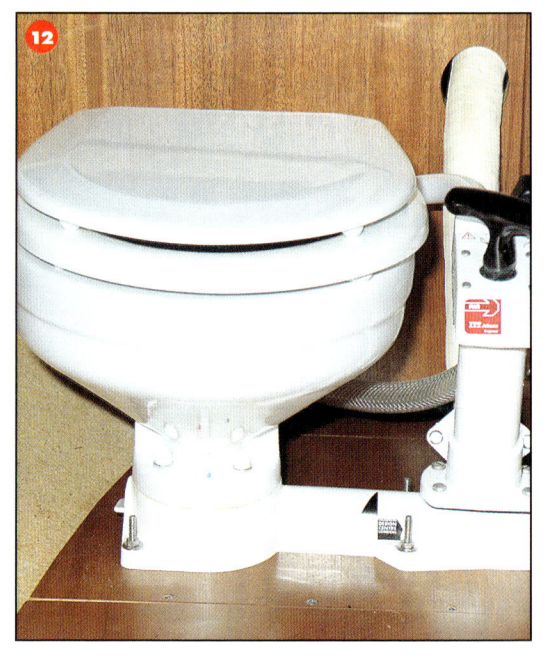

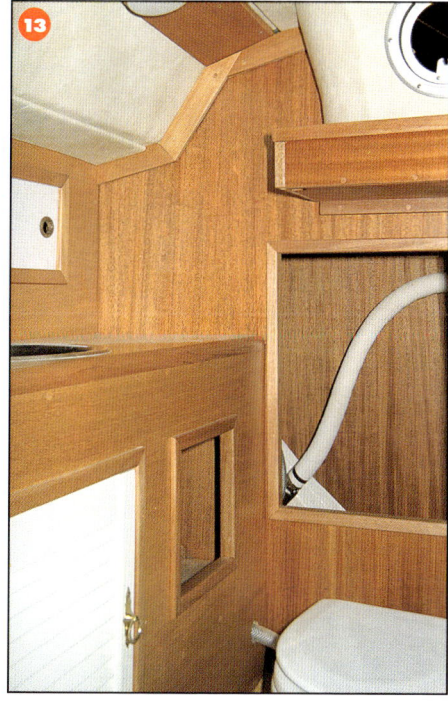

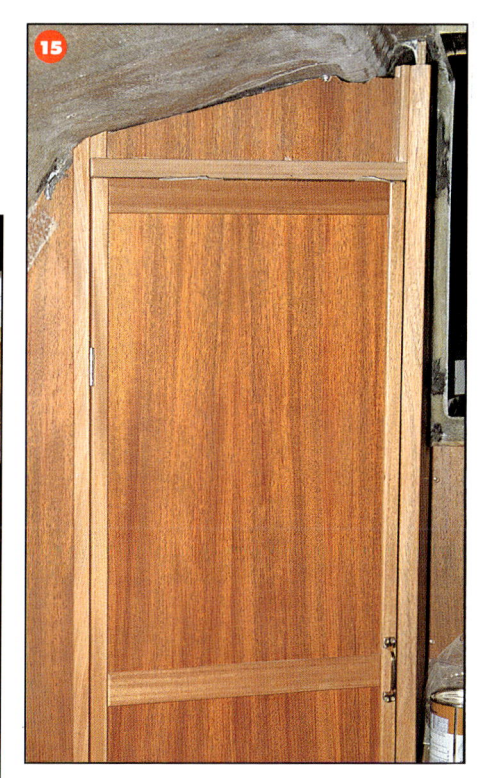

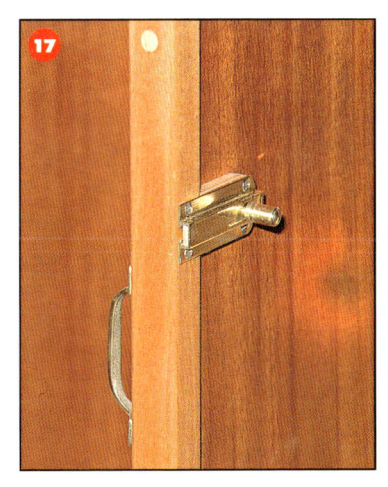

14 Fitting the door and frame has to be done with special care to make a good seal. Here a cardboard template has been made for the door head.

15 Pieces of plywood cut according to the cardboard templates for head and sides are glued in position.

16 The bottom part of the door which incorporates the sill has to be sturdy so this also is firmly glued to the floor. Dovetailing the ends of the sill into the frame stops it from shifting.

17 A handle is fixed to the outside of the door and the bolt is screwed to the inside.

75

18 The finished compartment has some elements of white to brighten up the colour scheme. The side panels have four coats of varnish and the sink surround has six. Interestingly, the white-painted louvred door was obtained inexpensively from a builders' merchant.

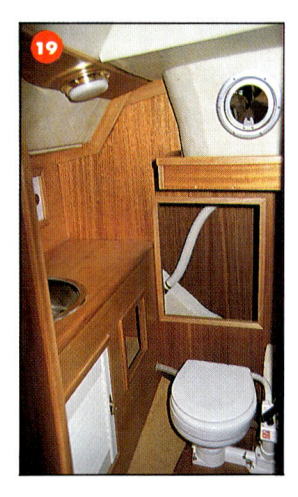

19 The finished compartment: the remaining surfaces are clad with vinyl sheeting which is finished along the edges with battens as described in the following chapter.

Finishing touches: covering the joins

This chapter is all about dealing with the junctions between the woodwork and the hull. In GRP-hulled yachts they are usually made with laminate angles that have to be covered by profiled mahogany battens.

When all bulkheads, built-in units and hull-connected parts have been installed, you can start cladding these edge connections. There is a choice of three methods.

In the first the connection is masked with plywood strips – a simple solution but one that is a little unsightly because the masking looks clumsy and 'boxy'. However it is the least expensive.

In the second method, the plywood strips are covered with vinyl (same colour and material as the rest of the headlining) and then screwed to the edge connection. This has the advantage that fitting need not be so precise because the plastic sheet covers up minor errors.

The best looking solution is the third option in which specially made profiled mahogany battens are accurately mitred and screwed on to the laminate. It is, however, the most expensive method since only very high quality mahogany can be used for the battens. Fitting is very laborious as every screw hole has to be carefully countersunk and plugged, but I chose this method, primarily for appearances' sake.

Before you can start fitting the battens, the laminate angle strip has to be prepared carefully so that the battens fit neatly. The laminate is ground to an even thickness using an angle grinder, and the strip is trimmed back with a small circular saw to the same width as that of the cutaway in the back of the profiled batten.

1 This is what the laminate jointing in a high-class sailing yacht usually looks like. The bulkhead is secured by means of three to five layers of matting on both sides.

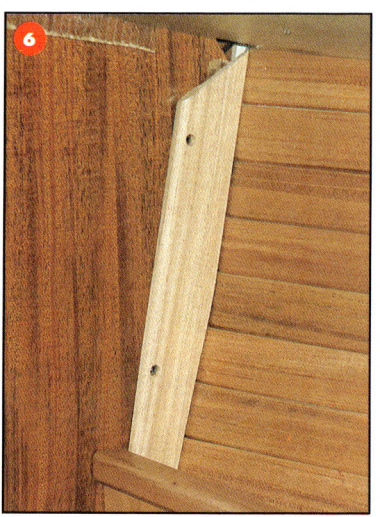

2 This small circular saw, which is easily fitted into the drill chuck, is extremely useful for cutting back laminate strips that are too wide. Blade life is about 2 metres of cut – so ensure you have sufficient spare blades.

3 The line of cut marked with a felt pen is followed carefully. You have to take great care here, because it's all too easy to damage the plywood underneath and weaken the bulkhead.

4 The sawn off laminate is detached from the bulkhead using a chisel. Take care here also, for if you go too deeply into the wood, strips of the top layer of ply could be torn out.

5 Here the laminate strip fills the recess provided for it in the back of the profiled batten. The screws go through the lower edge of the batten, where it bears directly against the bulkhead.

6 You start with the upright batten, its outer edge shaped to match the hull curvature. The mitre (at the top) halves the angle between deckhead panel plane and bulkhead edge line. It has to be exact.

7 The battens are fitted here but not finished. The mitred faces are glued with waterproof glue. The screws are all carefully countersunk. Make sure that the screw length is matched exactly to the bulkhead thickness!

8 Once all screws have been tightened, the plugs are stuck in with waterproof glue. Since they are very close to the edge, it is vital that tilt be avoided!

9 The plugs are chiselled level and rubbed down. The battens are then varnished with two or three coats.

10 If wiring is to be run behind the batten, a small recess must be milled where they come out. This is best done with a milling cutter fitted to the drill.

11 The skirting boards are fitted in the same way. Here the laminate is also first ground down level and, if necessary, trimmed back.

12 If you intend to have carpeting, the boards must be set high enough for it to slide underneath easily.

13 The exact bevel angle is obtained by 'parallel displacement'. First, cut the right bevel to the vertical wall, then hold the batten in position and mark as shown.

14 Where two different lines of battens meet, the edge must be cut back until the narrower batten just fits in.

Fitting profiled battens and panels as headlinings

Fashioning the headlining for the cabins is one of the most difficult elements of fitting out a boat. There are effectively no straight edges or flat surfaces, and the fact that you have to work above your head the whole time adds to the difficulty.

The ideal situation is where the part-finished boat has an internal headlining on delivery. First-time DIY fitters-out should, if possible, pick a boat which already has this inner lining – it will save much time and irritation. My boat required headlining, and this called for some careful planning.

Immediate questions to be asked are: light or dark colour? Do I want panels or profiled battens for visual effect? What do I do about electric wiring? How do I frame the portholes?

A light ceiling is generally considered to make a room 'friendlier' and, by an optical illusion, to offer more space. However, some hold the opposite opinion, based on the theory that a dark ceiling makes less of an impression and so is visually less significant. Of late, for instance, a trend has been to combine dark barrel-ceilings with light side walls to 'gain height'.

I, too, believe in that theory and, for that reason, amongst others decided on a relatively dark mahogany ceiling which contrasts well with the light side walls.

I chose the batten version, because you can then start from both sides and work towards the centreline. The use of large panels for deckhead cladding requires a large workshop and trying to do that sort of work on board is virtually impossible. Furthermore, you can't change the shape of panels in two dimensions; profiled battens are better in that respect also. If you eventually decide that you don't like the dark battens you can always paint them a light colour; they're quite suitable for that too. The electric wiring for lights and instruments is easily hidden behind the battens, but if you do that you should make a sketch of the circuitry for the 'ship's book'; within a year you may well have forgotten where the cables lie. I also made the edging for the hatch in the cabin from mahogany battens. An easier solution is to slide ready-made U-section strips of plastic over the sharp edges of the hatch frame – but it doesn't look as good.

1 Preparation: the ceiling is subdivided into two roughly equal-length sections; along the line between these, a strip of wood is screwed athwartships to which the battens are later secured. This subdivision of the length is absolutely necessary because work in the saloon with battens about 3 to 4 metres in length is impossible. Furthermore, every batten has to be fitted to the relevant bulkhead (no right angles); this division makes it easier to get the length right.

2 The fixing strip (light-coloured) must be thick enough to clear the bolt ends shown. That also allows you to run wiring as necessary between the battens and the deck.

3 Every batten must be fitted carefully against the relevant bulkhead. The angle grinder is used to ensure that the angle is precise.

4 You do this job working from outboard inwards, to get the V-shaped closing piece on the centreline. The wide (athwartship) gap halfway along is later masked with another batten.

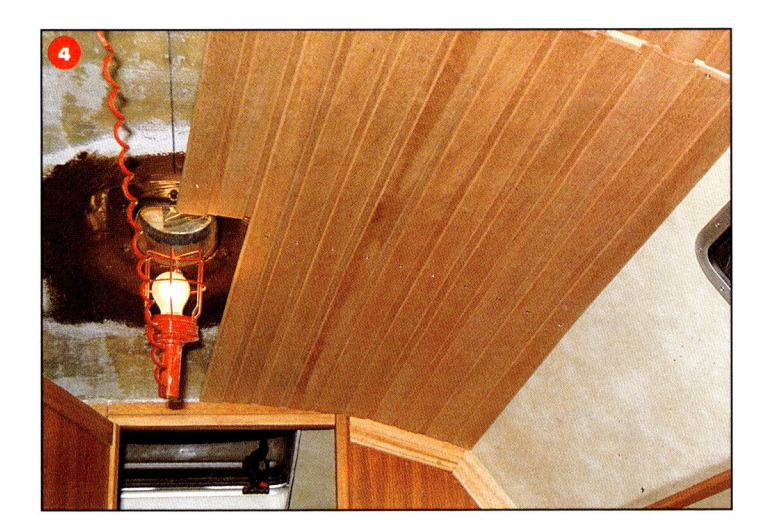

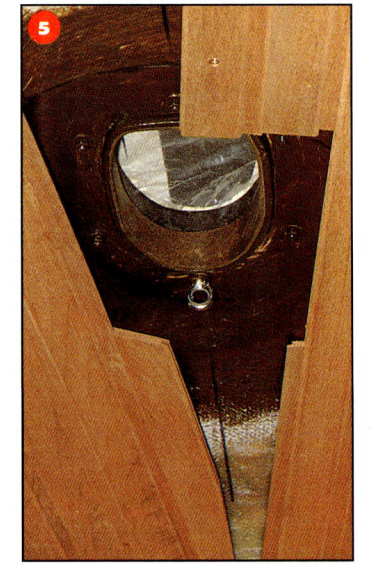

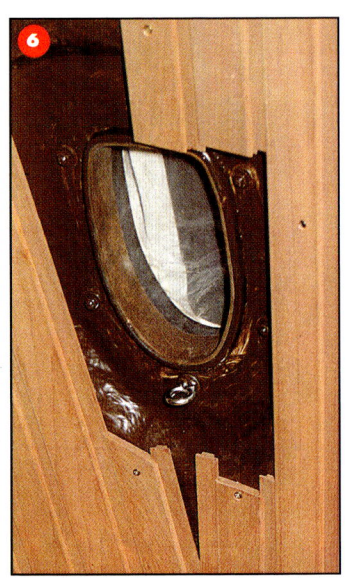

5 The mast centreline is approached from both sides. The marked centreline indicates how far the side of the batten has to be cut back.

6 This part of the fitting has to be done very carefully or you will get an ugly gap right in the middle. If you are reluctant to cut the battens straight away, you can first make some cardboard templates.

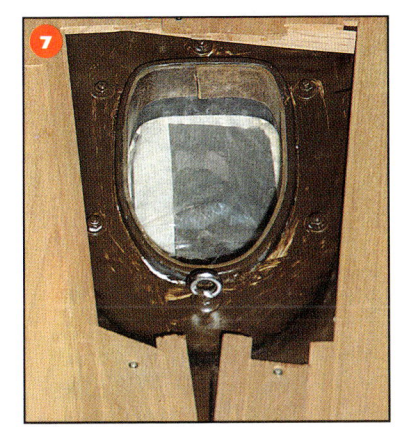

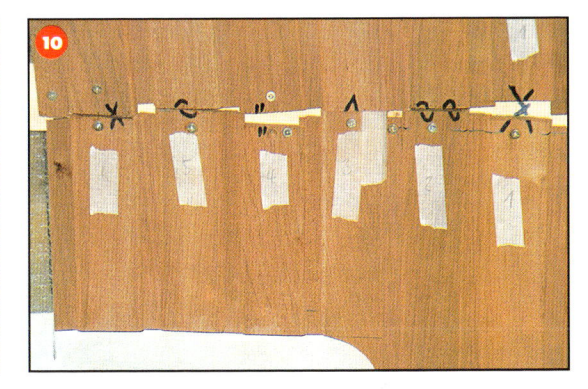

7 Here, profiled battens cover the whole of the ceiling, apart from where the mast comes through. Between each pair of wide battens there is a narrow, matching, tongue strip. The rim of the mast collar has a masking plate fitted over it later.

8 The battens around the hatch opening are cut roughly to length, numbered in sequence and marked.

9 They are held together with adhesive tape to keep them in the correct relative positions and cut to precisely the right length with the jig saw.

10 They are then screwed on again in exact succession. The pre-drilled fixing holes make it easy to find the correct position again.

11 The masking plate for the mast hole is initially screwed on from underneath. The correct position of the aperture is then marked from above through the mast hole.

12 Using a French curve, the shape is outlined precisely. It is shaped to allow for the eye-bolt for the tensioner.

13 The hole is then cut in the plate with the jig saw – from the underside so that the visible cut edge is neat.

14 With the drill sanding attachment, sand round the inside until all the cut edges are smooth.

15 Using the previously drilled holes, the masking plate is refixed in its original position.

16 The irregular gap between the batten ends midway has already been masked by a batten of adequate width.

17 When varnishing take care that none splashes on to the vinyl covering the sides, as it is not possible to remove this with solvent. A piece of cardboard is useful as a guard against splashes.

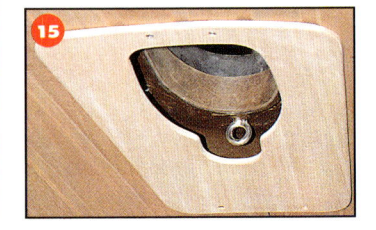

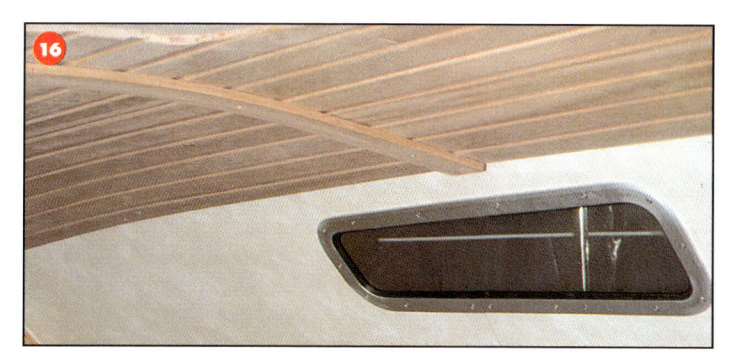

18 The cladding around the hatchway is made in identical halves from plywood 6 millimetres thick and screwed directly to the sandwich deck.

19 The completed border differs somewhat in colour from the battens. The frame for the hinged hatch, having been glued together, is screwed on from underneath.

20 The overall impression: the light-coloured sides and upholstery attract the eye downwards.

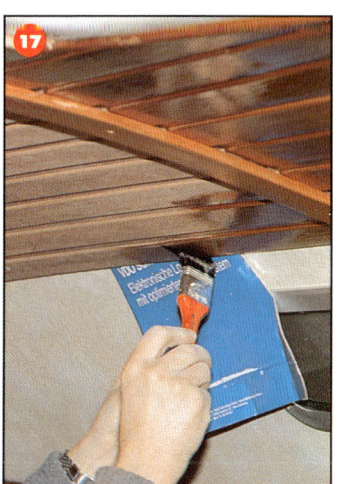

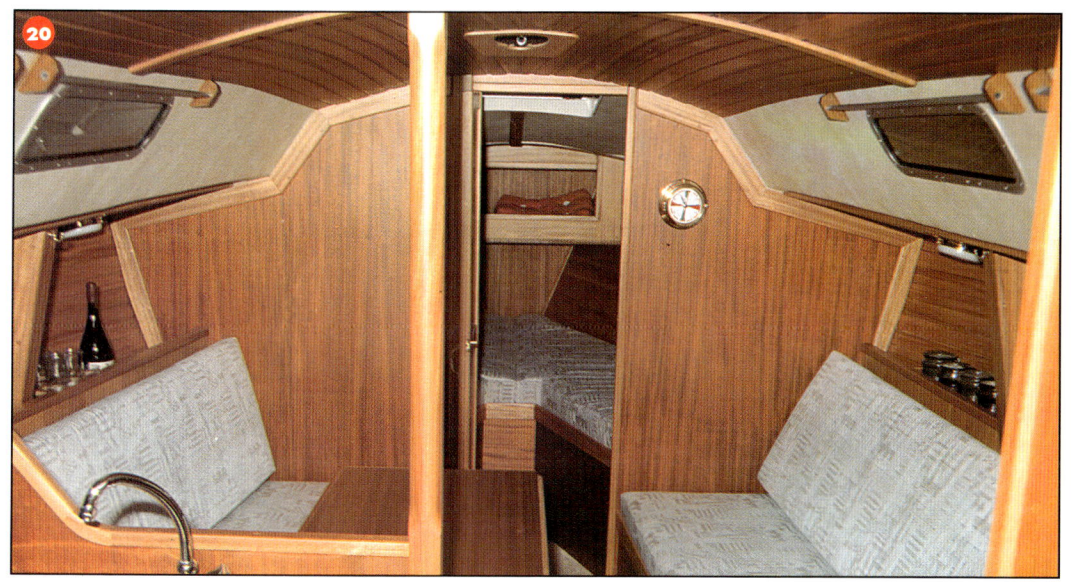

85

Gas installation

Anyone doing his own gas installation on board should take the greatest care. This chapter explains how to do it correctly.

Gas on board for cooking and heating has become a common feature in recent years. It has the advantage of being easy to use, clean and odourless.

However one must never forget that bottled gas systems are high-pressure so that inexpert installation or operation could lead to serious accidents. Thus anyone contemplating setting up the cooker, burner and pipe system himself should have sufficient professional knowledge and experience – or the work should be carried out by an expert who will also check that the system is totally free from leaks.

Freedom from leaks is the *sine qua non* for all systems, since any escaping gas, being heavy, runs downwards (usually unnoticed as you can't always smell it immediately) and builds up an explosive gas/air mixture in the bilges which can be ignited by the slightest spark. Hoses, pipes, valves and fittings should be obtained only from specialist suppliers who are familiar with the particular conditions existing on board. Cut-price gear from camping suppliers is unsuitable for use on board because of its low resistance to corrosion.

Installation must conform to British Standard 5482. Every owner should, on his own initiative, call for a check on his installation in accordance with this standard. Information on this can be obtained from authorised suppliers of bottled gas.

Copper pipes (8 × 1) should be used for all fixed piping and for the necessary flexible lengths attached to the bottle and to allow the cooker to be gimballed, pressure-tested hoses are used, connected by means of stainless steel or non-ferrous hoseclips. The pipes should be fastened to the hull with plastic clips which will not chafe them.

Do not even consider housing the gas bottle in the chain locker – that's the worst place you could think of. Salt water would quickly ruin fittings and connections and the chain running out would finish the job. An acceptable stowage is a specially-constructed GRP bottle chest, housed safe from water or shocks in the seat locker and with a vent/drainpipe overboard.

1 To cut a pipe, clamp it into the roller cutter so that it is just held in position.

2 The cutting disc is now applied to the pipe by turning the handwheel; the pipe being turned at the same time. The disc then cuts continuously under steady pressure until the pipe is cut through.

3 Using a triangular file, the slightly turned-in cut edge of the pipe is deburred. Check that the end is round and true.

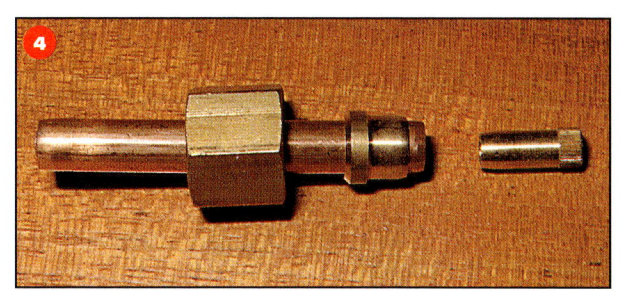

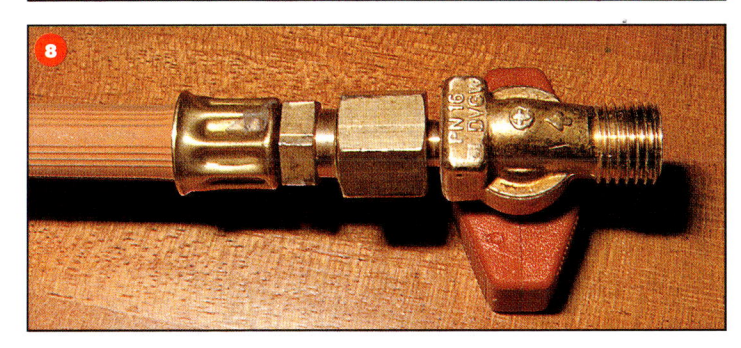

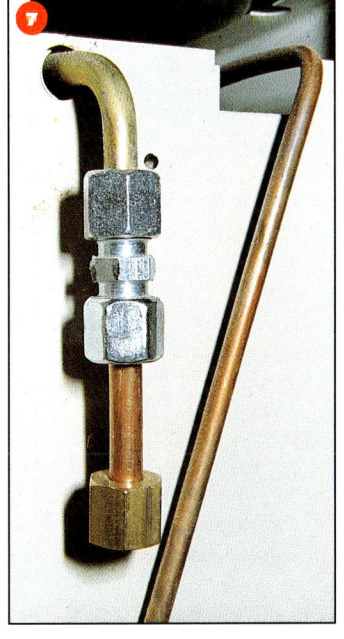

4 Compression joint components are, from left to right: the coupling nut, the olive and the backing sleeve. The brass backing sleeve is particularly important because it prevents the relatively soft copper pipe being squashed where it is under compression. The sleeve is driven into the pipe with a small hammer before the joint is made.

5 This backing sleeve is correctly positioned. The leading edge is level with the end of the pipe. Difficulties can arise if the pipe has not been properly deburred, so always ensure that the cutter cuts cleanly and then carefully remove any remaining burrs.

6 The olive must not be pushed to the end of the pipe before the joint is made. The illustration shows the correct position – the pipe projects about 2 millimetres. The olive *must not* be slid on the wrong way – the slimmer end always points towards the end of the pipe!

7 An example of a compression joint. The flexible hose could now be connected to this pipe stub with the coupling nut.

8 Quick-acting valves have the direction of flow marked on the back and must always be fitted accordingly (see arrow).

87

88

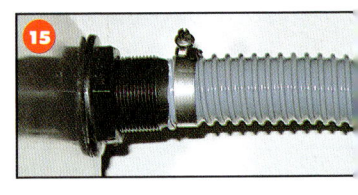

9 First make the joints between the quick-acting valve, the pipe and the hose, then fit the clip to the valve and drill the mounting hole.

10 The clip must be accurately and firmly located since operation of the valve must not place any strain on the joints.

11 The quick-acting valve should be mounted in an easily accessible position near the cooker so that it can be operated immediately.

12 A gas-fired heater unit in the locker seat. First install the equipment, then connect the system pipes. Pipe runs must always have generous curves as shown here.

13 The bottle in the GRP bottle chest. The fittings shown (in the direction of gas flow) are: bottle valve with coupling nut, pressure gauge, pressure controller and below that the electrically operated shut-off valve. This valve opens only if there is a 12V power supply, and so can be operated from the galley. A power failure will block the flow.

14 A twin quick-acting valve unit – one to the cooker, one to the heating unit. Fitted in this way, the two systems can be operated separately.

15 Hose (4 centimetres) for venting/draining the bottle locker. Any gas leaking from either the bottle or the pipes runs out to the transom.

16 Protection hood for the gas outlet in the boat transom. This will stop rain getting into the hose.

17 This is how badly sited fittings look after just one season. Corrosion caused by salt water and sea air is well advanced.

18 This can happen too: a brand new bottle leaks at the valve – soap bubbles identify the leak! It is advisable to check each bottle before connecting it.

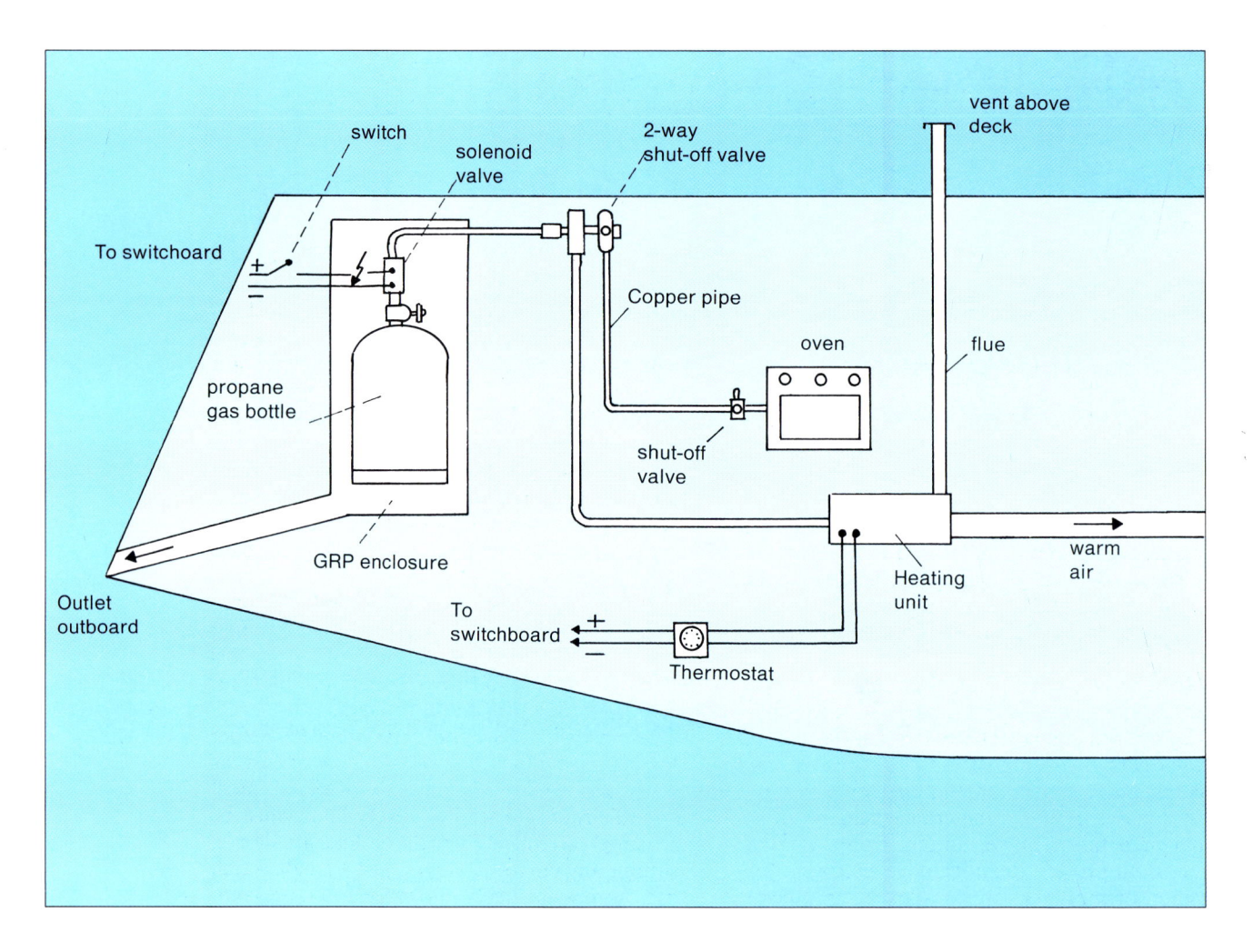

Gas system arrangement

The arrangement shown here is just an example, but basically only the dimensions change; the general layout is always the same. The gas bottle is inside a closed chest with a direct outlet outboard (in case a bottle should leak). On top of the bottle there is an electrically operated valve, remotely operable from the cabin, and from that valve the permanently-laid copper (8×1) pipeline connects to the two-way stop-cock which has one line to the heating unit and a second to the cooker.

A thermostat in the cabin controls the heating. Close by the cooker there must always be another master valve which should always be shut as soon as you have finished using the cooker.

Instructions for using the heating unit flue can be found in the manufacturer's operating manual. The run varies with different heating systems.

Upholstery for comfort and style

As you make your bed, so you will lie on it – this old saying applies also when on board. Sound upholstery is an important feature of a yacht especially when you plan to live on it for some time.

Selection of upholstery will be determined by the type of craft involved. A racing sailor fitting out his 'sportsboat' will give first consideration to the weight of the padding material and to water-repellent qualities of the covering. Comfort comes last. For his requirements a foam core with a 'volume weight' (that's how foam manufacturers indicate the density of the material) of less than 40 kg/m^3 will suffice. The material need not be more than 6 or 7 centimetres thick – since it's not meant for sleeping on for lengthy periods of time.

A suitable covering material would be either vinyl or a fabric made entirely from synthetic fibre. Both provide the advantage that a soaked cushion or mattress can be dried again quickly without taking it ashore. Cotton, wool and linen are totally unsuitable for this purpose.

A cruising yacht, intended to be comfortable, demands something different. The padding must be such that even after sitting or lying on it for a long time you don't feel the wood base underneath. Foam for this would weigh at least 50 kg/m^3, probably even more. That density guarantees – assuming a thickness of 10 centimetres – that even after hours of occupation you would not suffer discomfort by feeling the base boards. This applies particularly to seat cushions in the saloon, as with those used only for sleeping (forward and aft), the body weight is distributed over a large area. Therefore mattress thickness forward and aft can safely be reduced to 8 centimetres. A new technique allows comfort when sitting or lying down to be increased even further – the use of sandwich bolsters. These consist of a hard base layer and a relatively soft upper, for example 50 kg/m^3 underneath and $35\text{–}40 \text{ kg/m}^3$ on top. In such a combination two-thirds of the total thickness should be base material. Both layers are cut roughly to size, bonded together and then cut accurately, giving a soft and pleasant surface to sit or lie on with no risk of feeling the base underneath.

Before sewing the covering around the foam core, a layer of polyester wadding ($100\text{–}200 \text{ g/m}^2$) should be stretched and bonded on to it; this effectively softens hard edges of foam and prevents the covering material 'creeping'.

Before visiting the upholsterer or indeed before starting to sew (which I would advise against as these heavy materials tend to overload most domestic sewing machines), every bunk must be measured carefully. Where the outlines are simple, without any curves or slopes, just a small sketch with the measurements will suffice. For more complicated shapes you should make a template of thin cardboard. Any slope (bevel) in the side towards the hull must also be indicated accurately.

Having cut the foam cores to size, try them in place on board and if necessary trim them *before commissioning their expensive fabric covering*. I advise detailed marking of front, top, bottom, port, starboard, etc.

With regard to choice of material, you should consult a marine upholstery expert. He will know which materials have been a success afloat; anyone trying to economise here will regret doing so because within a single season inappropriate material will become wrinkled and unsightly.

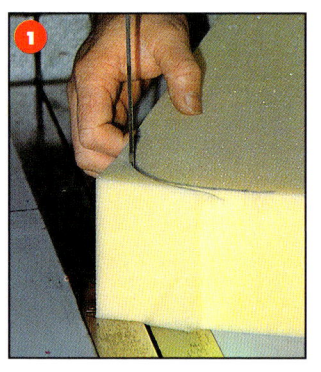

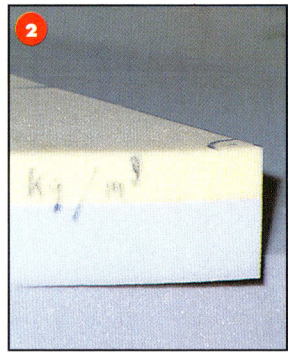

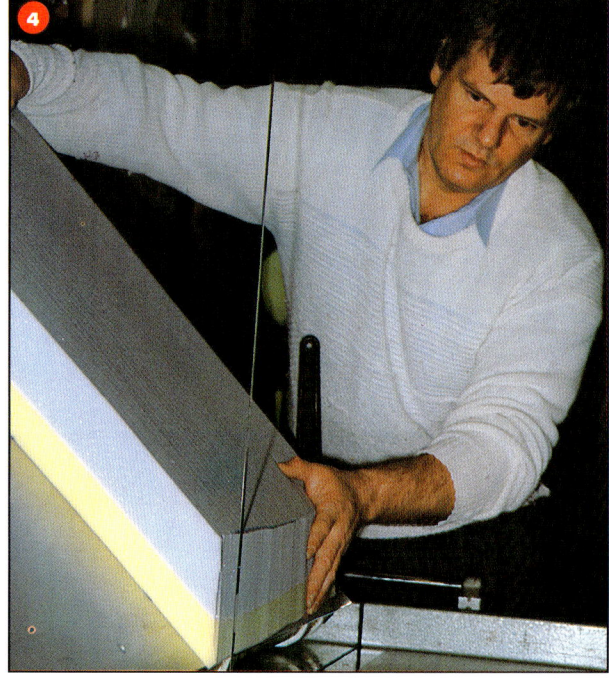

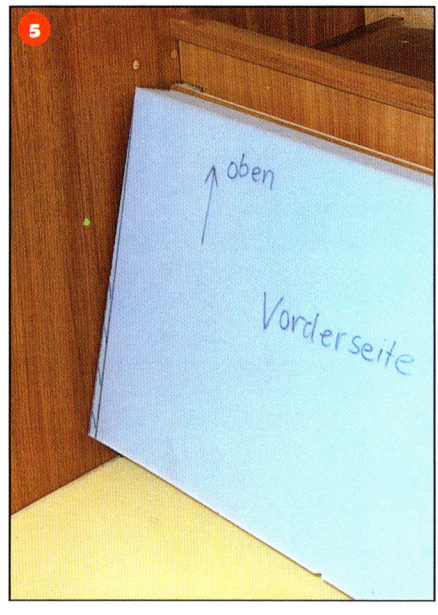

1 Foam for bunks used only for sleeping has a volume weight of about 40 kg/m^3. Thickness can vary between 6 and 10 centimetres depending on intended use.

2 To make a saloon bunk comfortable, you use a bottom layer of firm foam and a softer top layer, with the result that you sit/lie softly yet don't feel the base underneath.

3 Once the two layers have been bonded together, the precise outline is marked on and the whole cut to size with the special saw.

4 The angled face towards the hull must also be cut exactly right; if that angle is wrong, the cushion will slide about.

5 Make time to try out the foam on board; adjustments can be very expensive after the sewing is completed.

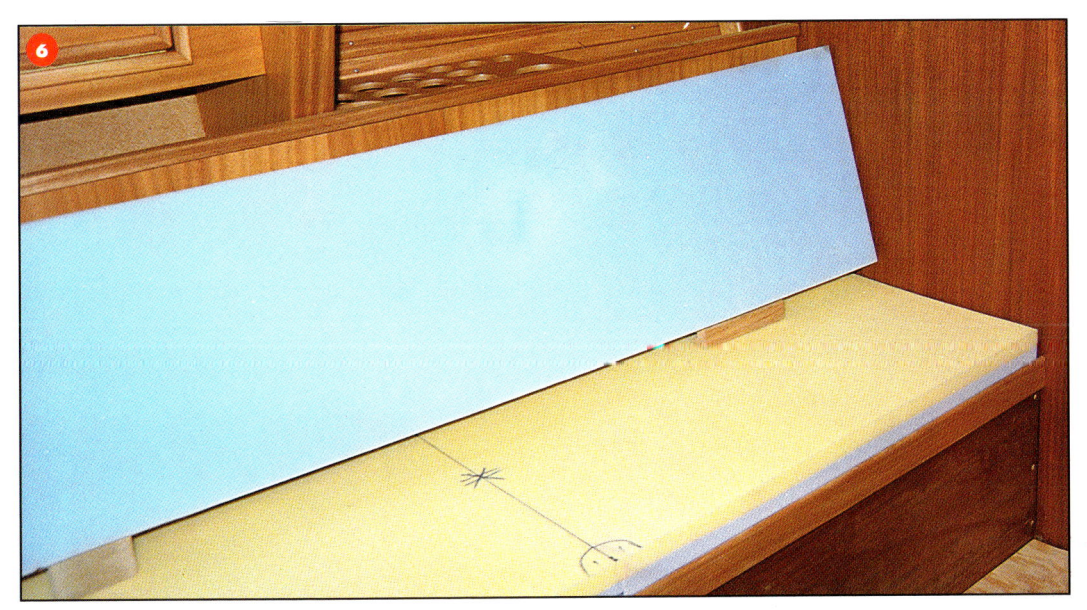

6 Backrests (4 or 5 centimetres thick) can be made in one piece while bunk cushions, which go on top of stowages, should be made in two pieces.

7 Don't leave the cushions with sharp corners; get the correct radiuses cut into the foam.

8 You will have better quality cushions if there is a layer of polyester wadding between foam core and the cover; this prevents the cover from creeping. Here, there is also a lining which I do not consider to be absolutely necessary.

9 The wadding-covered foam core is slid into the cushion cover which has a nylon zip along the back. That allows the cover to be easily removed for cleaning.

10 The edge seams can be piped – as shown in this example – or plain. Ultimately this is a matter of taste; there are no real practical reasons for preferring one or the other.

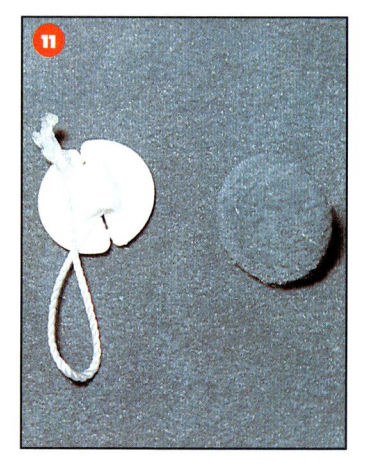

11 Buttons are additional cover-creep preventers, recommended especially for cushions with large surface areas. The counterpart for the underside has a small loop of nylon cord fastened to it.

12 The loop is pulled through the cushion using the special needle shown, and hooked to the underside of the button. The length of the loop should be about two-thirds of the thickness of the cushion.

13 A task that calls for dexterous fingers: jamming the end of the loop in the hook on the underside of the button.

14 A finished set of cushions. Those on the seat are left loose, the backrest cushion is hung from a Velcro strip the length of the bunk.

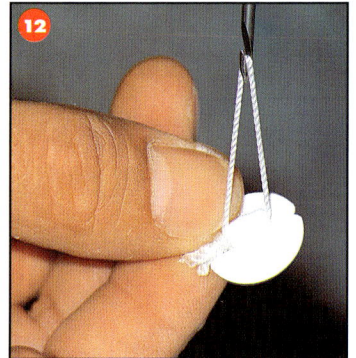

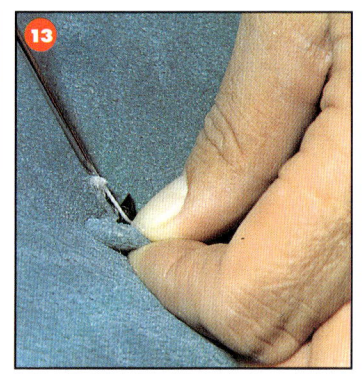

Installing instruments

Most yachts nowadays have both navigation and communication equipment. Sizes of equipment vary, of course, from manufacturer to manufacturer, but the method of installation is much the same for all of them. We give three examples here of how to install instruments on board.

It pays, before installing an item of equipment, to study its operating instructions closely because these contain details concerning not only installation but also functioning and the conditions, if any, of the guarantee. Inexpert installation can be a quick way of invalidating the guarantee.

Before you start installation, make a list of all the equipment you ultimately plan to have. Only in this way will you arrive at an allocation of space that allows enough room for every item (even if, for financial reasons, you don't intend to install all of them at once).

In order of importance I would suggest the following: compass, speedometer, echo-sounder, Decca Navigator (for northern regions) or Loran Navigator (for the Mediterranean), wind gauge, VHF set, RT frequency receiver and, depending on where you are sailing, a radar set.

Next to the compass, the speedometer is the most important navigational aid. Using an electronic Sumlog SL system as an example we show what you have to look out for. Almost every yacht nowadays has a Decca Navigator or Loran receiver. Using a Philips AP navigator set as an example we demonstrate how easy the installation of one of these is.

Fitting a lightning conductor is just as easy if you plan and install in good time, that is, before fitting out the cabin.

The wiring for the individual items of equipment should, as a matter of principle, be run in previously-fitted conduits. Wandering cables in any craft are not only unsightly but also dangerous. Wiring must never be left unprotected in stowages where stowed gear sliding about can damage them. And you should keep them out of any area where water or steam could affect them later (for example, bilges, chain locker, stern stowage). Apart from the VHF set, which is connected straight to the battery via its own fuse, all other leads are taken via the central fuseboard.

1 On the centreline, about half a metre ahead of the keel leading edge, is where the paddle wheel sensor for the speedometer should be fitted. That is where you can be sure of minimum turbulence in the incident flow. The circumference is marked out with a felt pen.

2 Either with a cup-shaped cutter or by drilling a ring of holes, the shape is made roughly. Hull thicknesses of up to 20 millimetres are not exceptional.

3 The webs between the holes now offer little resistance so that the middle portion can be knocked out with a hammer.

4 With a cylindrical milling cutter (fitted to the electric drill) the correct shape is neatly enlarged until the sensor will just go through (with about a millimetre clearance).

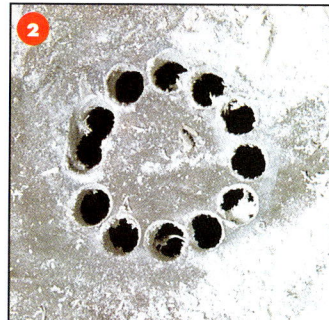

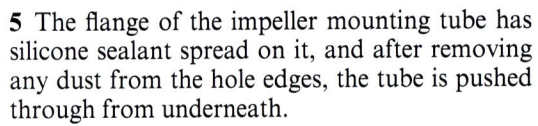

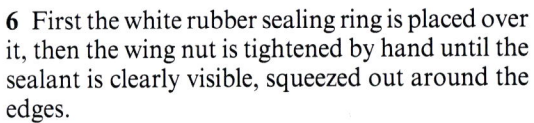

5 The flange of the impeller mounting tube has silicone sealant spread on it, and after removing any dust from the hole edges, the tube is pushed through from underneath.

6 First the white rubber sealing ring is placed over it, then the wing nut is tightened by hand until the sealant is clearly visible, squeezed out around the edges.

7 Now the body of the impeller can be inserted from above and fastened down with its coupling nut.

8 The connector in the lead is watertight, but it should still not be laid directly in the bilges.

9 Until you have finished running the lead from the sensor to the dial you should tape over the plug to protect it from damage and dust.

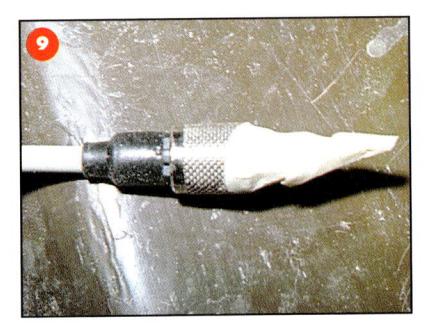

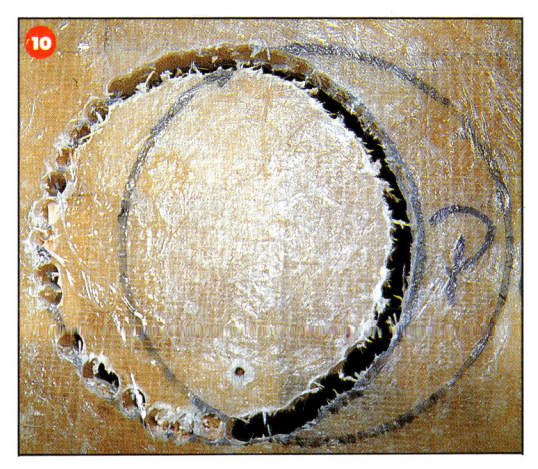

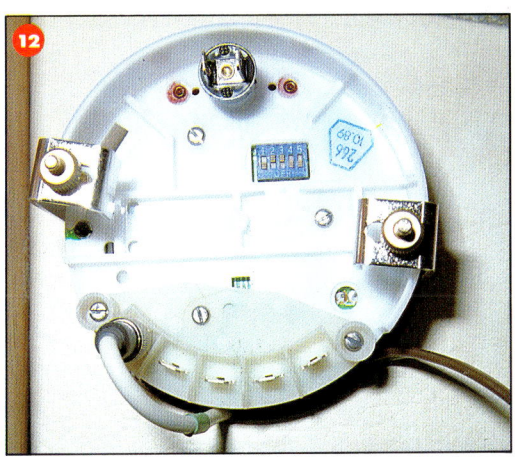

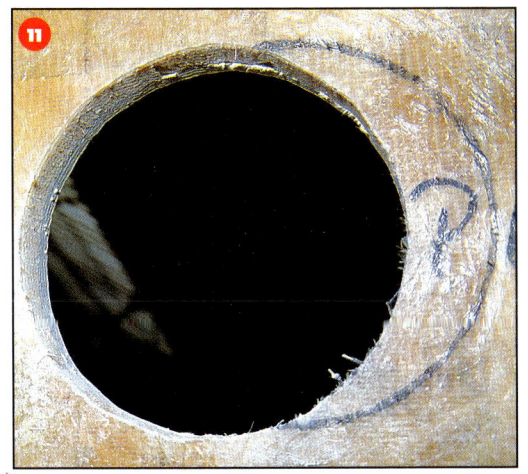

10 The hole for the dial is cut from the outside inwards to avoid the gel coat being sprung off (seen here from the inside).

11 The hole is enlarged to the required size with a cylindrical milling cutter. The instrument should have a 2 or 3 millimetre gap around it.

12 The instrument is pulled inwards by means of its clamps, so pressing its flange against the outer surface.

13 A rubber seal between flange and outer surface makes the joint watertight. No additional sealant is needed if the surface is smooth, but if it is not, sealant may be used to fill the gaps.

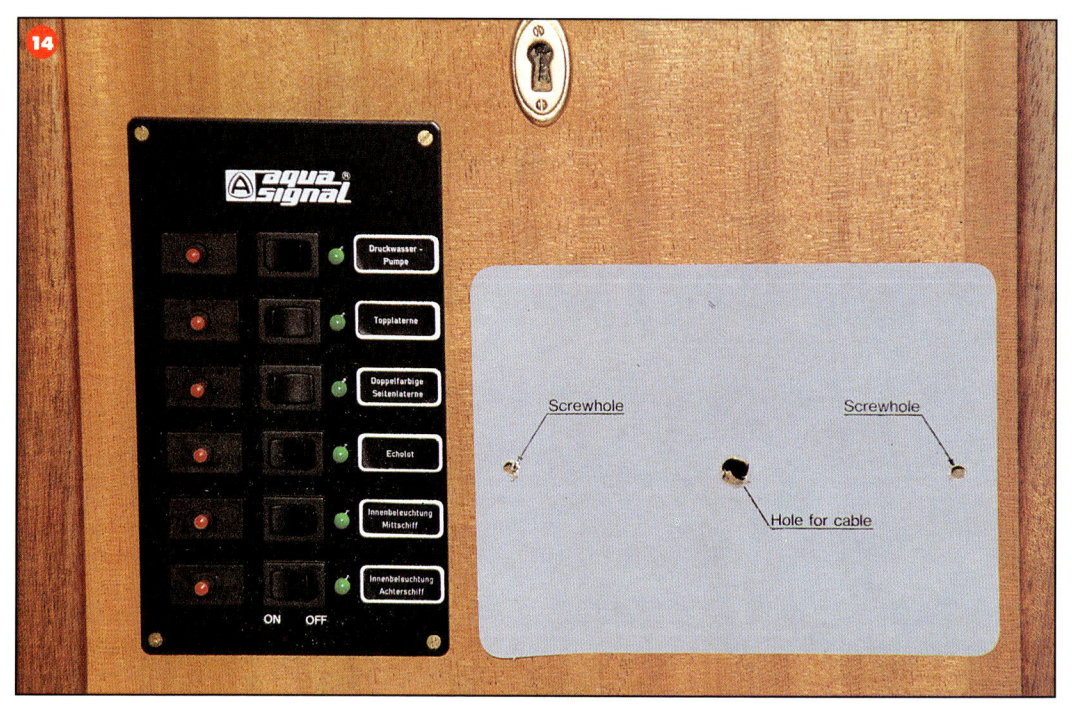

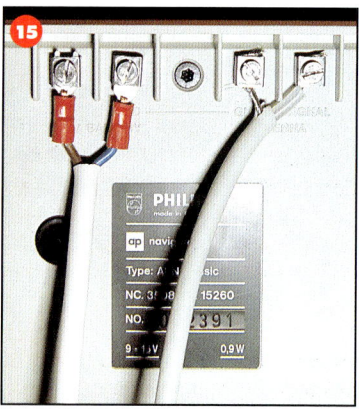

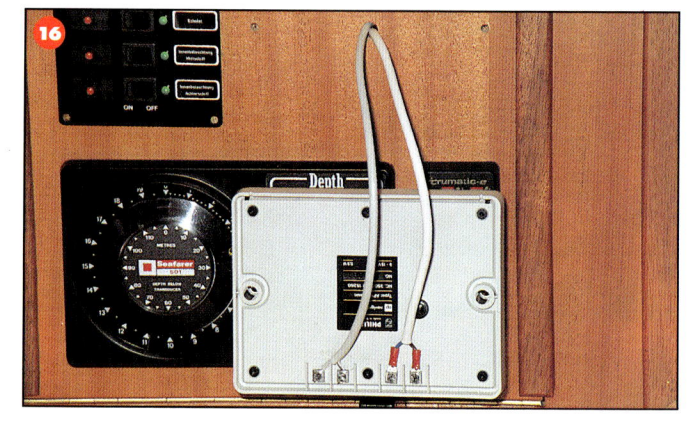

14 Installing the AP navigator: the drilling template supplied with it is stuck in the preselected position to allow the holes to be drilled accordingly.

15 12V supply and aerial terminal are clamped firmly to the back of the instrument.

16 The drilling template is removed and the leads are pushed through the central hole.

17 Two securing screws fasten the instrument to the panel. It can be installed in the cockpit if preferred provided that the casing is watertight.

Fitting a lightning conductor

It may be rare for lightning to strike a yacht, but if it does happen and the yacht hasn't got an effective conductor you have to reckon on significant damage. The crew, of course, is in as much danger as the craft.

Only someone who has already sailed in a thunderstorm, or has seen lightning strike, can appreciate the importance of this installation. According to statistics, a lightning strike on a sailing yacht is quite rare, but if you are the one struck it is small comfort to know that many other yachts will get through unscathed.

If you are doing your own fitting out the amount of work involved in providing effective protection against lightning is fairly small. Difficulties only arise if you try to carry out the installation later, when everything else is already in place.

The best means for linking the various fittings is braided copper strip as used in the motor industry for earthing. This strip is especially flexible and therefore easy to lay. Suitable terminals are fitted to the ends of the leads and clamped to the fitting.

Yachts with non-metallic (wooden, GRP) hulls and metal rigging plus a bolted-on metal keel are earthed (or rather, 'watered') as follows: connection provided below decks for – forestay, shroud chainplates, backstay, guardrails and mast. The leads are taken as directly as possible to the keel bolt. Masts extending down through the deck are connected directly to the keel bolt.

Yachts with internal ballast require a large area 0.3–0.5 square metres) copper earthing plate, since the ballast itself obviously is no use for earthing.

Should lightning strike, there is the risk of flashover, or of inductive influence, affecting all electrical or electronic equipment in the vicinity of the lightning conductor, possibly resulting in considerable damage. This risk can be substantially eliminated by providing effective potential equalisation. That involves providing metallic connections between the metal casings of all items of electronic equipment and from these to a lightning conductor lead. The engine and any metal fuel or water tanks should be included in the equalisation. The connecting leads should be copper and at least 4 millimetres square in cross-section.

Shrouds or stays used as aerials need a pair of insulators fixed at top and bottom, each pair being at least half a metre apart.

1 The lightning conductor. The chainplates (holding the shrouds) are linked to the keel bolt by a copper strip.

2 The copper strip is led down towards the keel laid flat against the hull. If necessary the strip can be glued down.

3 The site where all the leads come together. Ideally forestay, backstay, shrouds, mast and guardrails are all earthed to the keel bolt.

4 Optimum lightning protection for a GRP yacht, retro-fittable: mast and all shrouds and stays are linked to the keel by leads of adequate cross-section. An (imaginary) protective cone has been created. (*Drawing: Astrid Witte/YACHT*)

5 How to run the leads for a lightning-conductor system: difficulties arise where the aluminium mast is just standing on the deck (left). Leads are run from it to port and starboard, down to the keel bolt or to earthing plates on both sides of it. (*Drawing: Astrid Witte/YACHT*)

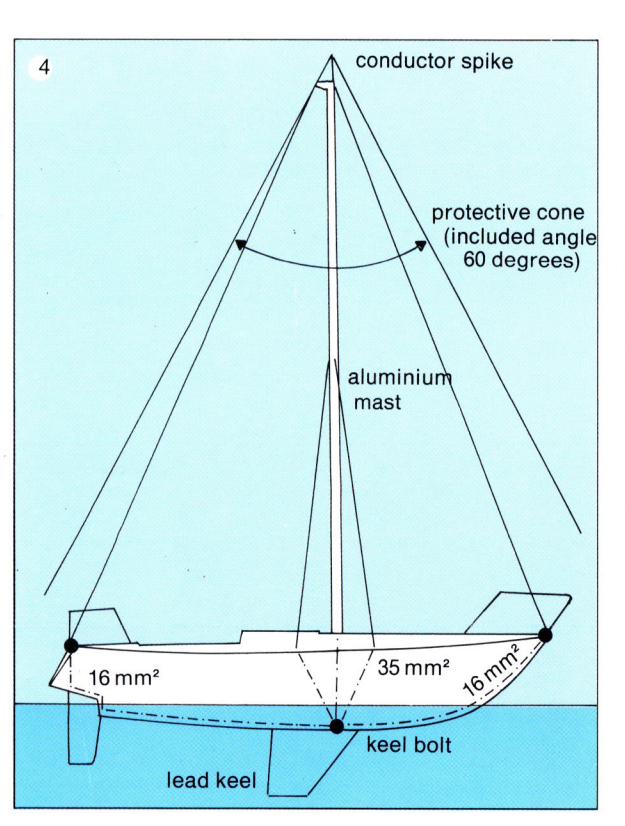

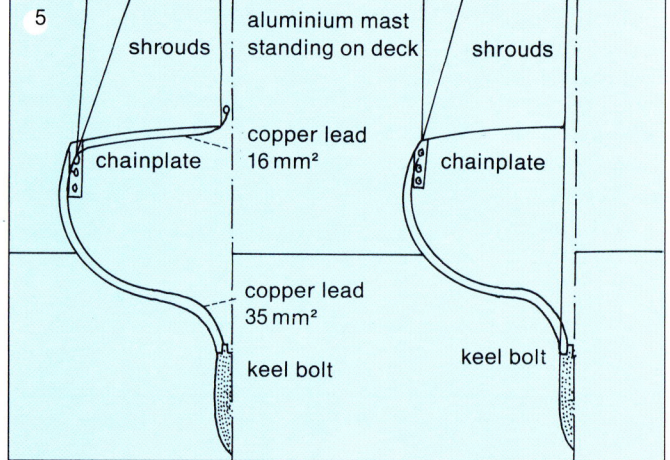

Soundproofing the engine compartment

Sometimes sailors do have to resort to the auxiliary engine – even if they'd rather not! Whether the reason is lack of wind or the fact that it's blowing from the wrong direction, the noise from the engine compartment is never enjoyable. If, additionally, the machine is inadequately encased and poorly soundproofed, your cruise may not be as enjoyable as you had hoped. In this chapter we show you how to teach your engine to whisper.

The engine of a sailing yacht is bound to have a fairly lowly place in the planning order. The designer does determine the centre of gravity and indicate precisely where it is to be sited, but installation and soundproofing are often left to the boatyard. Soundproofing may be given low priority and suffer through cost-cutting; this will not necessarily be apparent when the prospective owner makes his decision to buy. Only later, after the launch, does the engine noise manifest itself.

If the noise is really unacceptable it is still possible to soundproof the engine compartment at the fitting out stage; fortunately, a wide range of different soundproofing materials are available.

First, let us take a look at the basic principles of noise generation and suppression on board. Even at the installation stage, things can be done that significantly lower the noise level.

When mounting the engine and its accessories, a 'soft' mounting should be aimed for; that is, one with rubber inserts – shock absorbers – between base and engine to absorb the vibrations. In this way, structure-borne noise, the noise transmitted from mechanical components to the entire vessel, is greatly reduced. If, on the other hand, the engine is rigidly fastened to its base the hull can act as a resonator, making any noise reduction practically impossible. Unfortunately, there are some shafting layouts that make rigid mounting of the engine unavoidable and in particular long shafts with two rigidly fixed bearings.

If possible the exhaust silencer should also be rubber-mounted to eliminate another source of structure-borne noise.

The outdrives, which have become increasingly popular in recent years, have a special advantage in this respect. On top of the ease of installation for the yard, there is the advantage that the engine, transmission and shafting are all in one unit and supported by one integral shock-absorber. Obviously structure-borne noise levels are exceptionally low in this case.

1 The nap-finish mat of this flame-resistant plastic has a self-adhesive coating on the back, covered by a thin protective film which is not removed until the mat has been accurately cut to size.

In addition to the form of noise discussed above there is also 'air-borne noise'. Sound waves strike the engine compartment bulkheads; these must be absorbed, that is, converted into another form of energy. This is ideally achieved by applying open-textured materials which have a very rough surface. On one hand this refracts the noise, and on the other enlarges the surface area causing the sound waves to be absorbed.

In dealing with structure-borne and air-borne noise, there are two different reduction methods, namely silencing and soundproofing.

Silencing involves the use of suitable components such as rubber engine mountings or substantial walls for the engine compartment. Soundproofing on the other hand involves the use of material to prevent vibration for structure-borne noise, and absorbent layers for air-borne noise to dissipate the sound energy. So in practice there are four elements to master.

Adhesion

For fixing soundproofing materials, most manufacturers offer a single package adhesive which is applied to both surfaces; these are then joined after waiting for a short while to allow the adhesive to partially dry. The disadvantage of using such adhesives is that in small engine compartments special ventilation is needed to speed up evaporation of the solvent. However, for special situations, solvent-free adhesives can also be obtained on request from the suppliers of the material.

Some manufacturers make mats which have a layer of adhesive on the back protected by a film which has to be removed before application.

Should you decide to line the engine compartment in this way, bear in mind the following basic rules:
- Line all accessible surfaces as carefully as possible
- Seal all cracks and gaps well
- Don't line the bilge region
- Don't attach the lining to areas near to parts of the engine which get very hot.

2 When gluing this self-adhesive mat in place, it has to be right first time. It is not possible to slide it around later. The base surface (wooden) must be clean, free from grease, and dry. This method of gluing, with a self-adhesive backing, is a lot simpler than using adhesive containing solvent.

The electrical system

The cable system

Cables in GRP hulled yachts are usually laid in laminated ducts or PVC conduits. You must decide at this point whether to use cables or single-core leads as used in car wiring. For yachts up to about 10 metres, the latter solution is suitable if you are prepared to use one lead, correspondingly thicker, for the (negative) return from a number of separate circuits. In larger boats and those with wooden or metal hulls, cables are installed on cable trays and secured with clips or straps at 20 to 30 centimetre intervals to prevent them from sliding about as the boat moves, and being damaged by scuffing.

All wiring on board should be twin core for safety. The heart of the electrical system is the distribution board, the terminal for all incoming and outgoing cables. Each facility (ie lights, navigation instruments etc) will have its own fuse and each individual circuit will have its own fuse and switch.

Generally the best form of cable connector on board is the screw-clamp terminal, with non-corrosive screws. Soldered connections should be avoided as they tend to break off. If you use spade terminals, they should be those with crimped connectors.

Direct current generates magnetic fields which causes magnetic compass error; such errors cannot be compensated for because they depend on the strength of the current (for example, electrical sheet winch on load or idling), and of course on whether the circuit is live or not. Therefore, cable runs must be a suitable distance from compasses. For a cable with a load of 10 amps, you should allow a distance of 0.8 metres. Supply and return leads for feeding electricity to magnetic systems, for example, for compass illumination, should be twisted together.

Copper wire connected to a steel terminal in a damp atmosphere will often give rise to corrosion at the connection point. Unless this is rectified the electrical equipment concerned may fail to work.

Cable cross-sections

So that cables and leads do not heat up unduly (due to current flow) their cross-sections have to be matched to the current consumption of the individual circuit at the distribution board and fused accordingly. In the distribution board, circuit breakers can be used as safety cut-outs.

Apart from twin core wiring, adequate earthing is also required together with protection from corrosion, by means of a sacrificial anode, of the electrical connections. The drawing shows the principles of a combined lightning- and corrosion-protection system and twin core cable run.

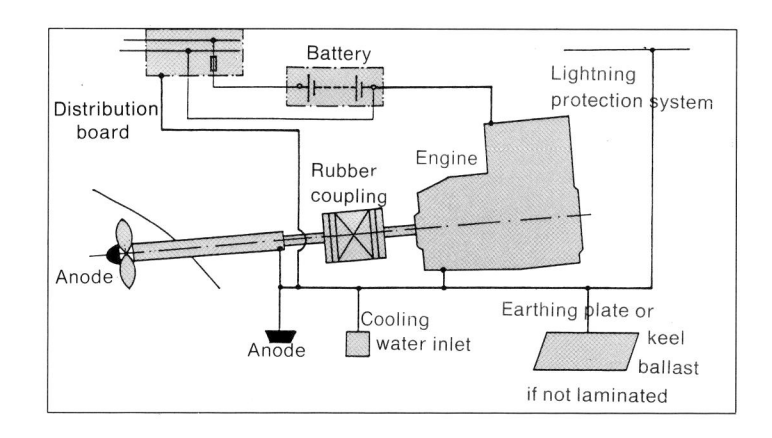

It is important to use adequate cable size (ie cross-sectional area) for low voltage circuits otherwise there will be a drop in voltage, particularly on long runs.

For further advice on electrical installation, refer to *Boat Electrical Systems* by Dag Pike and *Boatowners' Mechanical and Electrical Manual* by Nigel Calder; both published by Adlard Coles Nautical.

Standard conductor cross-section mm²	Single core cable Maximum permissible current A	Single core cable Fuse rating A	Twin core cable Maximum permissible current A	Twin core cable Fuse rating A	Three and four core cable Maximum permissible current A	Three and four core cable Fuse rating A
1.5	12	10	10	10	8	6
2.5	17	16	14	10	12	10
4	22	20	19	16	15	16
6	29	25	25	25	20	20
10	40	36	34	36	28	25
16	54	50	46	36	38	36
25	71	63	60	63	50	50
35	87	80	74	63	61	63
50	105	100	89	80	73	63
70	135	125	115	100	94	80

Table for determining the conductor cross-section for various rated current strengths. The fuse rating is always less than the permissible current.

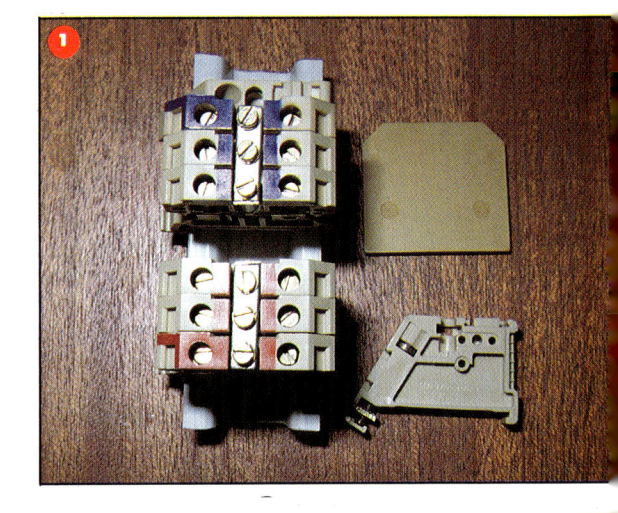

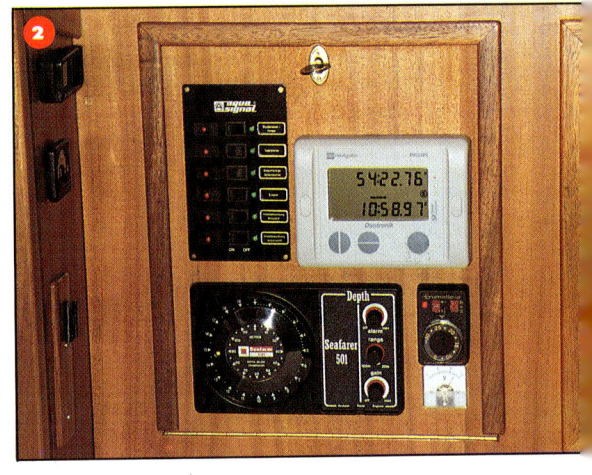

1 Individual circuits are brought together at and supplied from block connectors, such as these. Individual connectors, as many as are needed, can be fastened on to a DIN rail.

2 The completed distribution board with fuse panel and integral switches, LEDs, and circuit breakers, echo-sounder, Decca Navigator, heating thermostat and voltmeter. All items of equipment are connected to the back of the fuse panel. Details of the wiring are shown in the *Wiring Diagram* opposite.

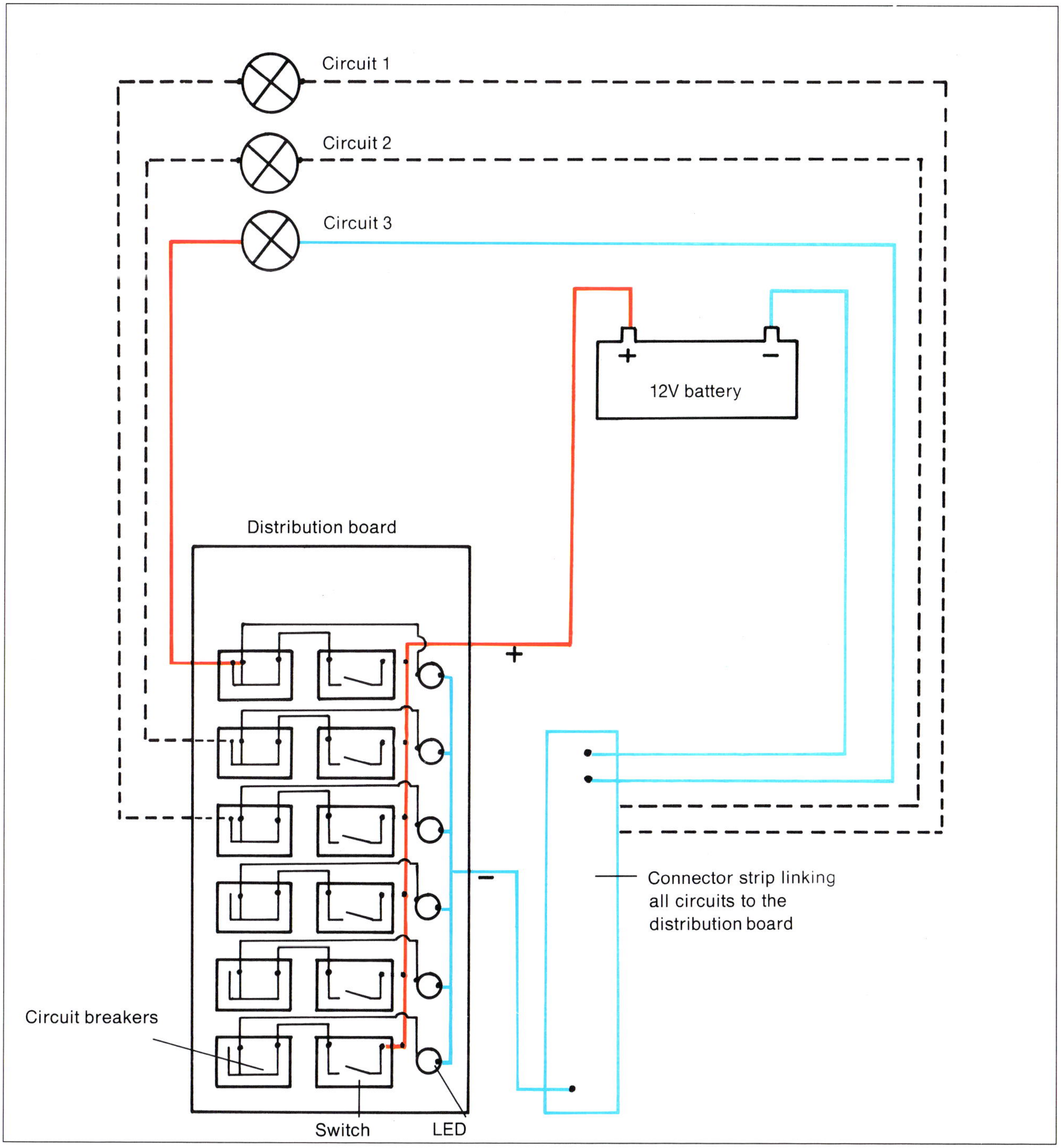

Circuit 1
Circuit 2
Circuit 3
+
−
12V battery
Distribution board
+
−
Connector strip linking all circuits to the distribution board
Circuit breakers
Switch
LED

Varnishing

The final attractive appearance of the yacht interior will depend very largely on the successful application of the varnish.

Two different kinds of finishes are usually required when fitting out a yacht; the GRP surfaces are primed and coated with polyurethane paints, preferably the two-part type; wooden surfaces are treated with clear varnish.

The GRP surfaces must be painted with reasonable care, but a 'curtain' in the bottom corner of a stowage isn't going to catch the eye straightaway and can be excused. The wooden surfaces, however, are a different matter; varnish runs down the door of the saloon will ruin even the most splendid piece of woodcraft. I am not going to recommend various makes of varnish, but remember that good varnishes for interior use can be obtained from the building trade as well as from chandlers, often cheaper too. Before buying large quantities of a specific product, make a sample trial run on some offcuts to establish whether you are satisfied with the flow and the covering power of the varnish. The choice of gloss or matt varnish is something left to the individual, but you should bear in mind that achieving a really good effect with gloss varnish calls for a steady hand and a lot of rubbing down – you will get on faster with matt!

1 You have to rub down before *every* coat – initially with coarse grain glasspaper (100 or 180); later between coats with 260 to 360 grain. Don't buy the cheapest; better quality paper lasts a lot longer.

2 Wide, flat surfaces are smoothed easily and quickly with an orbital sander. First use a coarse grained paper, then finish with fine. The larger the number on the back of the paper, the finer its grain. Always wait until the previous coat of varnish is absolutely dry before rubbing down.

3 Limit the area to be varnished by means of adhesive strips; use masking tape for rough edges, film for fine outlines.

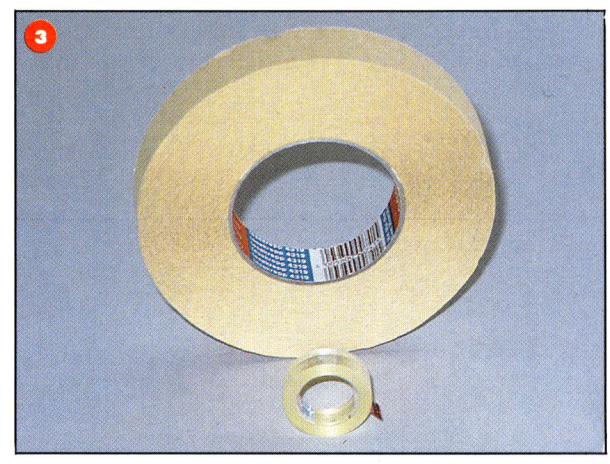

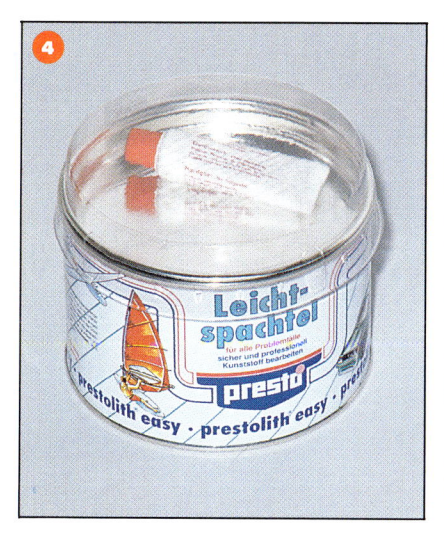

4 GRP surfaces, and floorboards which are to be painted, should first be made smooth with mixed compound filler.

5 Before buying large tins of paint, try it out in small quantities first. Only when you are satisfied with it, buy larger quantities.

6 For the priming varnish coat, add and mix in about 30 per cent thinners so that the varnish can penetrate as far as possible into the raw wood. For subsequent coats you can continue to mix in up to 10 per cent, depending on the varnish (check the flow).

7 There is a huge range of different paint brushes. Buy good quality brushes from a specialist for the best results; make sure you get the right type for the job.

8 Foam or fleece rollers are particularly suitable for applying the top coat to the GRP areas, but for varnishing, I prefer to use brushes because these give a better flow into nooks and crannies.

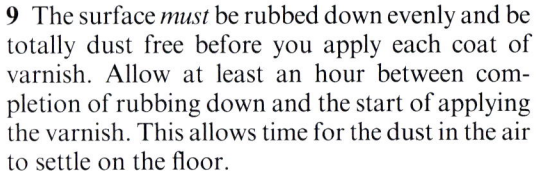

9 The surface *must* be rubbed down evenly and be totally dust free before you apply each coat of varnish. Allow at least an hour between completion of rubbing down and the start of applying the varnish. This allows time for the dust in the air to settle on the floor.

10 When varnishing along an edge it's easy to shield the adjoining surface with a small piece of cardboard. You don't have to cover everything with masking tape.

11 If you have to apply varnish to hollows, don't overfill the brush and press it in very carefully.

12 Freshly-varnished mahogany at first looks two-tone – with alternating light and dark areas. It takes time (about a whole season) for ultraviolet radiation to blend the colours more closely and tone down the overall effect.

108

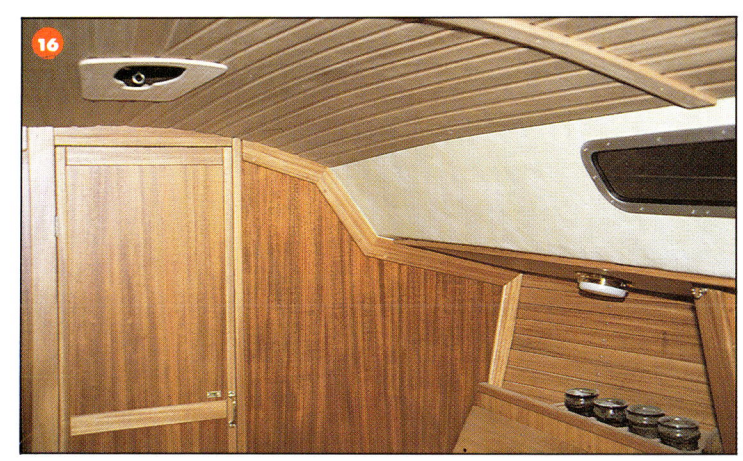

13 Here you can see how the colour of the wood appears to vary before any varnish has been applied. So always do a test with the varnish before joining pieces of wood of differing origin.

14 After the first coat of varnish, you can see whether the colours of different pieces of wood match. Subsequent coats don't change the colour significantly.

15 Every kind of wood reacts differently; in this case the colour change is particularly pronounced. A trial is therefore essential.

16 The headlining unvarnished – the wood looks almost pallid because the depth of the grain has not been brought out.

17 It takes no more than the first coat of varnish to bring out the attractive tones of the wood. When rubbing down between coats you should use a sanding sponge to get right into the grooves. During and after each varnishing session, ventilate thoroughly!

Fitted carpets

I consider that a yacht isn't truly cosy down below unless a carpet matching the decor has been laid on the cabin floor.

The most suitable flooring for racing and charter yachts is plain wood – either ply panels or ply strips – which are easy to clean and maintain. But if you want a bit more luxury and warmth in the saloon you should cover the cabin sole with a carpet of highly waterproof and rot proof material – this is no place for natural fibres.

I have divided the cabin sole into two parts: aft, below the companionway where you more often stand in wet shoes and where, from time to time, water gets splashed from the galley – here there is to be wood strip flooring; further forward in the seating area, below the bunks, I intend to lay carpet.

In order to achieve a pleasing overall appearance, the carpet has to be trimmed as accurately as possible to avoid ugly lumps and gaps. As the shape of the sole is quite complicated, a cardboard template is an absolute must, the carpet then being cut to this shape.

1 What you need: a batten, sharp scissors, a pencil, cardboard, adhesive tape. The cardboard should be about 1 millimetre thick and lie really flat.

2 The various pieces of cardboard are taped together and the outer edges trimmed so that there is no gap between the bunk sides and the other butting edges.

3 When the cardboard template has been cut to the right shape, it is placed on the back of the carpet and the outline pencilled on to this. The straight edges are cut with a carpet knife; the curves with the scissors. Carpet cut this way can then be laid precisely between all the cabin fittings.

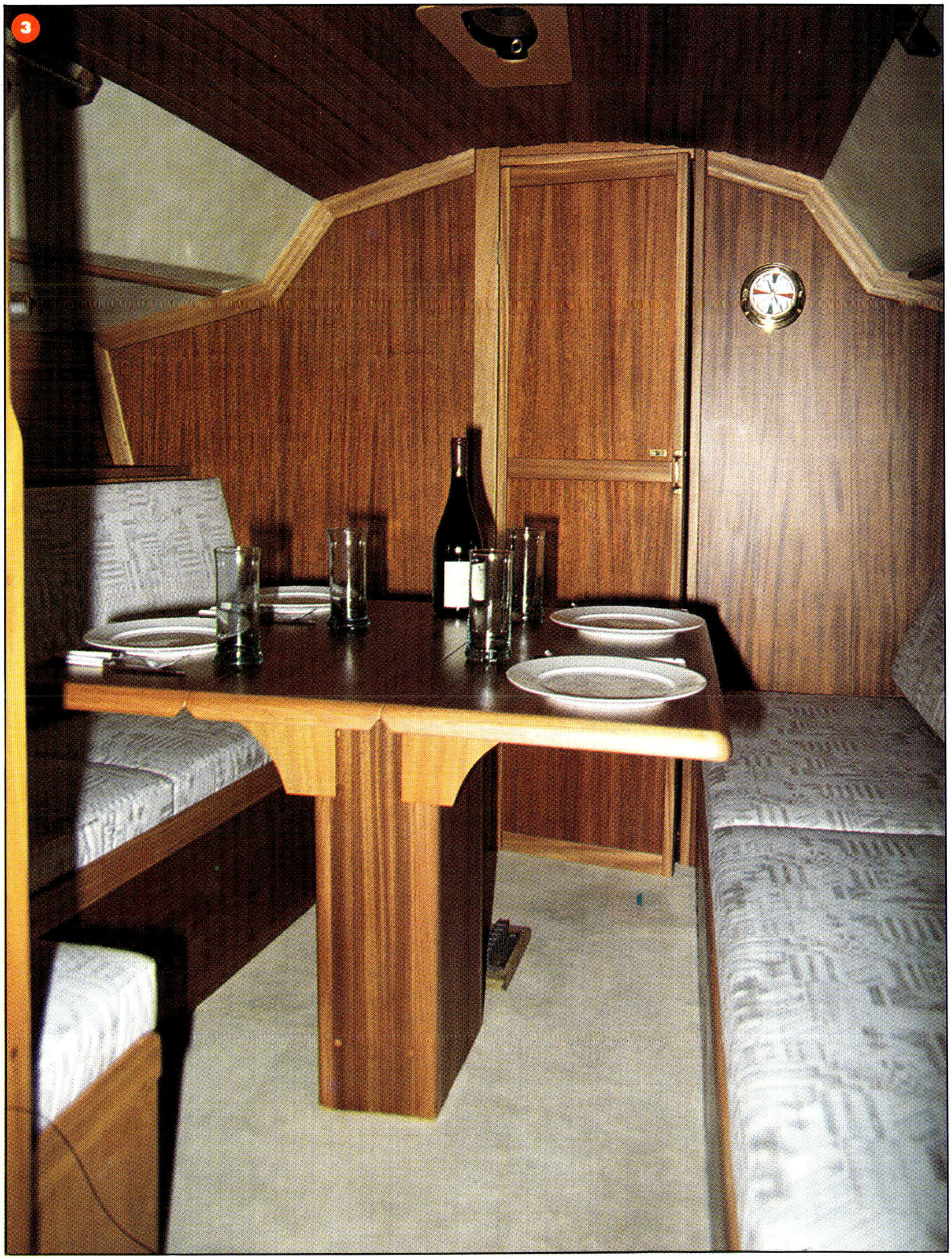

Perspex doors

Sliding doors are very useful for small lockers and cupboards. If made of plywood they are simply cut out of a suitably sized sheet, rubbed down and varnished. When making them from Perspex, however, there are important points to be observed.

Perspex doors look good, are easy to keep clean, don't need to be varnished and can be transparent or coloured as required. I prefer transparent doors, particularly for the galley because even with the doors shut you can see from outside where to find the mustard and where the gas lighter is! Handling items inside the cupboard is also easier because there is always sufficient light.

The cupboard in the heads has white Perspex for appearances' sake and because you don't necessarily want to reveal the contents of the cupboard to every visitor. There is no significant difference when cutting and finishing transparent or coloured Perspex, but scratches in the former show up more, so careful work is needed.

Depending on the size of the door, you use 4 or 6 millimetre thick material, the guide grooves in the frame being always 1 or 2 millimetres wider – no more than that, otherwise the doors will rattle too much in the grooves.

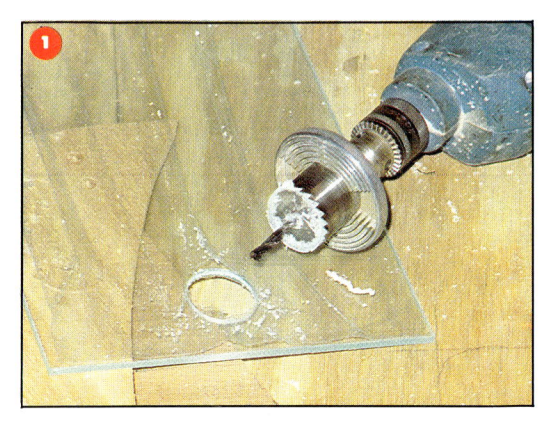

1 When purchased, Perspex has a layer of protective film on both sides. Don't remove this until you've finished working it. When cutting finger holes always lay an old piece of plywood flat underneath and drill through to that, to get a clean edge to the hole in the Perspex.

2 So that the film on the Perspex slides more easily, and to stop it getting damaged, stick strips of adhesive tape on the table. It is then much easier to slide the door past the grinding wheel at an even speed to get a smooth, clean edge.

3 Run the grinder at high speed and press the Perspex against the wheel very gently. The material must not be allowed to get hot, because owing to its poor thermal conductivity, it melts very easily.

4 Perspex sliding doors in a galley locker. To remove the door, it is pushed hard up into the upper guide groove and tilted to clear the bottom one.

5 These white doors add to the appearance and conceal the contents of the cupboard from view – a better solution in the heads.

6 In principle it's enough just to smooth the edges of the finger holes with glasspaper, but it looks better if you glue in a wooden finger-hole edging (using compound glue).

Perfection in design and colour

I have gathered these 'masterpieces' from various boat shows to demonstrate how professionals deal with problems of detail. We amateurs can't expect to achieve this sort of success at first go – but as you know, 'practice makes perfect'.

Designers and creators of fashionwear don't live in a vacuum – on the contrary, the influence of hints from competitors and from customers, and of the trends of changing tastes, show up in their products. It's just the same with boats – you need to keep looking around. I have kept my eyes open for particularly good solutions to problems of detail, not just to copy them, but rather as a provider of ideas. By kind permission of the Aphrodite yard (Sweden), the Martin boatyard (Radolfzell), Conyplex (Holland), Grand Soleil (Italy) and Satas (Sweden) I was able to take these photographs of what are, in the truest sense of the word, 'masterpieces'.

1 A successful solution of the problem of how to deal with a headlining in a sailing yacht. The traditional character has been maintained, but using modern materials. The mahogany makes a good contrast with the light surfaces.

2 The contrast between light headlining and dark wood furnishings is also pleasing. I feel that the light surfaces should not be chalky white but rather slightly tinted.

3 An example of the 'genuine' traditional deckhead with glued-on beams and white enamelled plywood. It is expensive, but gives a beautiful classical finish.

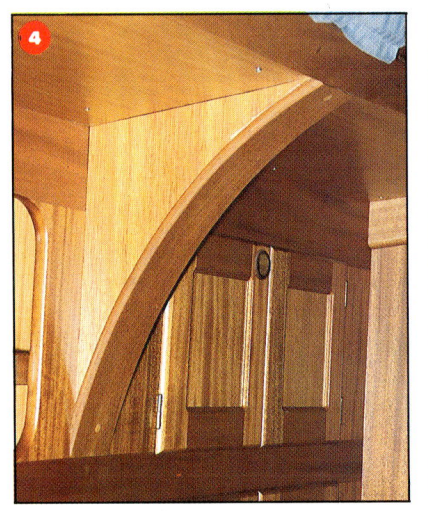

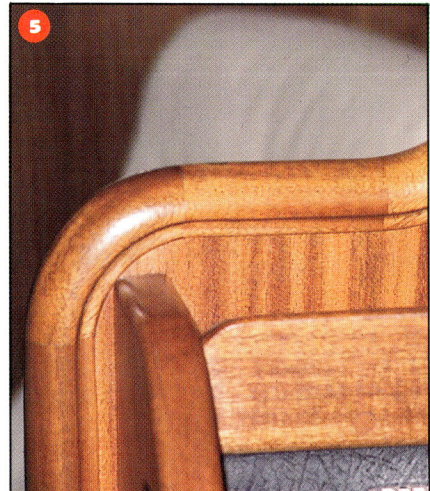

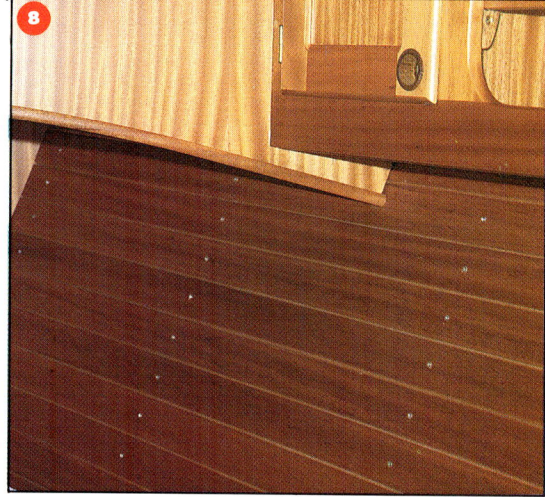

4 An attractive curve – another way of concealing chainplates below deck. Rounded arches don't look massive and are comparatively easy to make.

5 The perfect handrail. Not only functionally correct but also beautiful to look at and touch. The colour of the wood is well-chosen, too.

6 The fully exposed pillar. The solution shown here is very expensive for the one-off build. It is machine prepared, but quickly set up.

7 A complicated corner. Unless the battens are fitted together absolutely perfectly, a corner like that can look a mess. It is best to either avoid such corners or treat them with extreme care.

8 The shape is acceptable but the coloration leaves something to be desired. However ultraviolet rays will, in time, make the strong colour contrasts largely disappear.

9 A very clever way of making a door – but you have to have the correct machinery to do it. DIY-ers should steer clear.

10 Perfect in every detail. It's not often nowadays that you find solid wood drawers. In most the body is plastic and only the fronts are made of wood.

Selecting the sails

There comes a time when anyone who has fitted out a yacht has to face the question of selecting the right set of sails. There may be a standard set for the type of boat, in which case it is only a question of deciding the quality of the material. Otherwise the sailmaker has to be given precise measurements in order to make the sails.

My personal advice is that if money has become short towards the end of the fitting out (and I have never known it to be otherwise), don't order just any old cheap set of sails which won't last very long, but see if you can get a second-hand set instead. These are often very cheap and will do well enough for the first year.

If you do have sufficient cash for a new set, then start with the mainsail and order the rest later. Get as many sailmakers as possible to give you a quote (autumn is the best time to ask) so that you can decide which is the best.

I opted for a relatively expensive material: a Triax cloth from Polyant, made up by Dickow-Segel, which, in effect, consists of three layers – a very strong foil in the middle reinforced by a layer of fabric on both sides.

1 The sail material under the magnifying glass: in the middle the ultra-strong foil; on both sides a layer of fabric – here separated for the benefit of the camera.

2 In this macrophotograph the big difference in strength between warp and weft can be clearly seen.

3 In this direction the material tears relatively easily because the thin threads of the weft are only intended to hold together the strong threads of the warp.

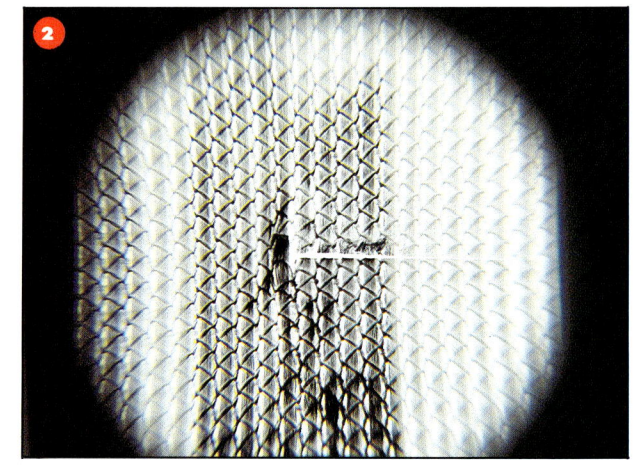

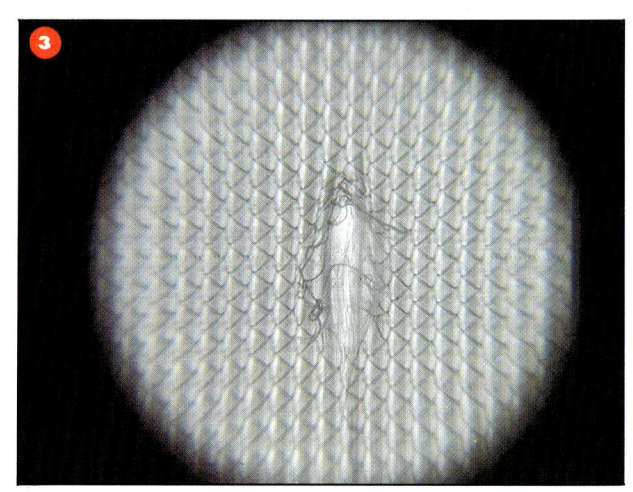

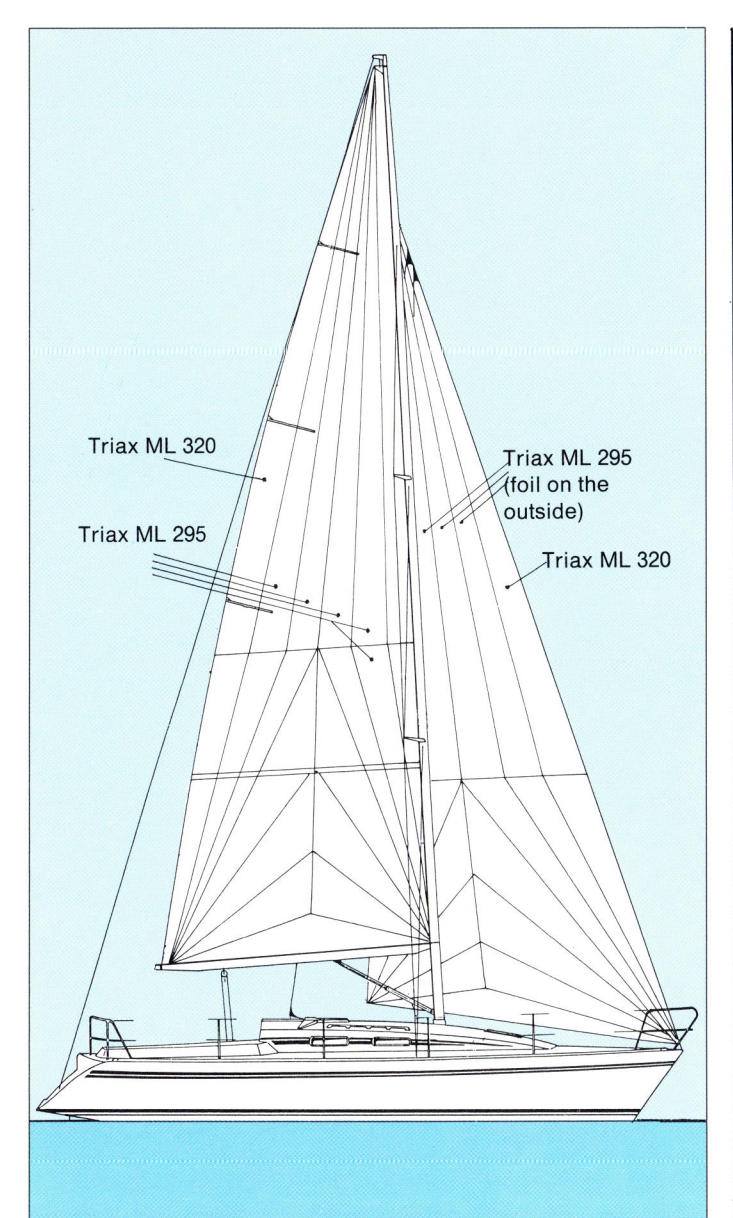

4 The cut of the Diekow sail. The figures include the cloth weight in grammes per square metre.

5 This kind of sail material can stand high stress only in one direction – that of the strong warp threads. Thence the triradial cut – the pull is radial from the centre outwards.

119

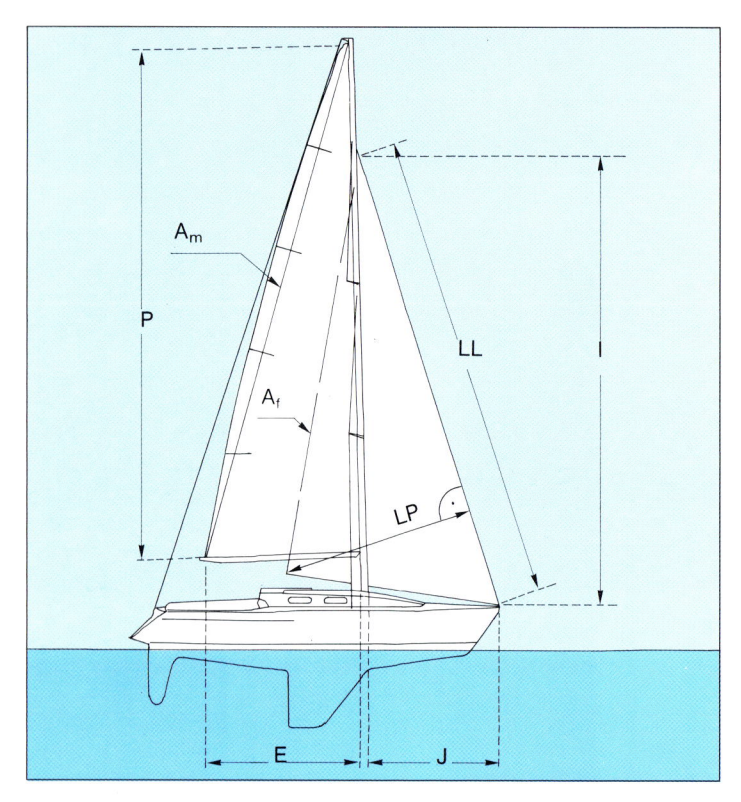

If you do not want, or cannot get, a standard set of sails for your boat you will need to do some very accurate measuring before placing an order with a sailmaker. That is particularly important if you designed the rig yourself and there is no standard sail plan available. From the drawing shown here you can see exactly which dimensions are vital when ordering sails. It is preferable to measure once too many times than once too few, and better still, get someone else to measure as well and compare the results. If the sail has been incorrectly cut, there's little to salvage. Discuss all the details with your sailmaker as making sails is a much more complicated job than people generally think, and tell him also how heavy your (fitted-out) boat is, as this is an important criterion for the sail designer.

These are the dimensions the sailmaker requires in order to make the sails

P	Mainsail luff
A_m	Mainsail leech
A_f	Foresail leech
LP	Clew to forestay
LL	Luff
E	Mainsail foot
J	Mast leading edge to forestay
I	Height of forestay mast fitting above forestay deck fitting

5 The highly stretch-resistant material sets beautifully and it's very easy to adjust the profile.

6 This mainsail has only one batten stretching right across it – precisely where the sail is deepest. That means that the sail sets in the desired shape even in very light winds.

Laid teak decking

It took 150 hours to lay the deck of this 9 metre sailing yacht, strip by strip. The result is something worth seeing and the time and hard work was well worth while.

The first step: the calculations

If you do decide to lay a teak deck yourself to improve the looks of a GRP yacht, you should understand that there is a price to pay later. A teak deck may look superb but it is not so easy to maintain when in regular use. Also you need to work out whether your boat will be able to take the extra weight of the teak. For my part, I thought it worth laying a new deck on a five-year-old Show 29.

The first thing to find out is, how much money one can save, as an amateur, by doing the work oneself, and to what extent one will still require the services of a boatyard.

To be clear from the start, provided that you possess a decent set of woodworking tools, and a reasonable amount of skill you can do all of the jobs that are required for laying a deck. Basically, as long as you have a proper set of instructions it is just a matter of plain hard work. The working conditions required are a dry, well lit workshop or boat shed, temperature not below 10°C and a 220 volt power supply.

The master craftsman shows the way

From an experienced master boatbuilder I obtained some expert advice and some first hand knowledge of procedures. He was finishing the deck of a 10 metre seagoing cruiser in the same workshop, so I didn't have to go far at any time for advice. I shall describe every stage of the work in chronological order and shall indicate where special problems may arise. One of the most important bits of preparation is the rigging of scaffolding with sturdy planks around the yacht because it's no fun working whilst kneeling on the deck all the time. While at work on the wood you could just about get by without scaffolding, but later, when gluing down the strips, you simply must have it. The height of the scaffolding should be such that the toerail is roughly at waist level. Provision of this all-round gangway is the only really essential preparatory work. Generally, a normal set of woodworking tools is all you need and the only special tool required is the plug drill obtainable from specialist tool shops.

When all the deck fittings, chainplates, etc, have been removed you can make a start with smoothing the surface. Use a disc sander fitted with 60-grain sanding discs which will produce a surface that is both smooth and adhesive-friendly. Ensure that you roughen the gel coat but don't go right through it. At this stage make sure that any potential obstacles are removed; that extra effort will pay off handsomely later when you're laying the strips. There is nothing worse than having to work round a fitting left in position.

When you have got the deck smooth and clean, you can give thought to the laying scheme – obviously something to be decided in advance. Generally, there are two options – either you run the strips parallel to the toerail and adjust the butts at the superstructure, or you start with the strips running the full length next to the superstructure and adjust the butts at the toerail. There is no hard and fast rule for this – it's simply a matter of taste.

1 Originally, the deck was covered with a layer of rubberised cork put on with a compound adhesive. When the covering has been stripped away, adhesive is left on the GRP deck.

2 Using a large disc sander, the whole of the surface is smoothed back to the gel coat. Unless all the adhesive is removed, problems with water leaking through can arise later.

3 Deck fittings must be removed as far as possible, otherwise later it will be difficult to lay the strips neatly. For holes you cannot later re-drill from underneath templates will be required.

4 The well-seasoned teak planks are first cut roughly to size to provide a flat contact surface. The wood had been stored beforehand for about three weeks at room temperature and was dry enough to cut.

5 The planks are next cut into rectangular bars. Care must be taken to see that, when these are later cut into strips, the annual rings of the trunk are as near as possible perpendicular to the ends.

6 If the annual rings in the strips are not perpendicular, later, when the deck gets wet, the strips may warp instead of just expanding horizontally in the desired way.

7 The bars have now been cut into strips; the substantially perpendicular annual rings show up quite clearly. If the strips don't distort during cutting, that is a sign of good quality wood.

8 A milling machine cuts the tongues, the strip being automatically fed past the circular saw. Only tools made of a special alloy are used; ordinary tool steel would not be strong enough for cutting teak.

9 The finished strips are tongued all along one side, which later ensures that the seams between adjoining strips are all the same. You can also use strips tongued along both sides, but these tongues are then half as wide.

123

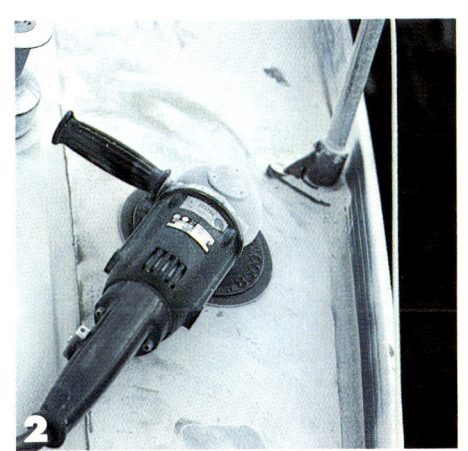

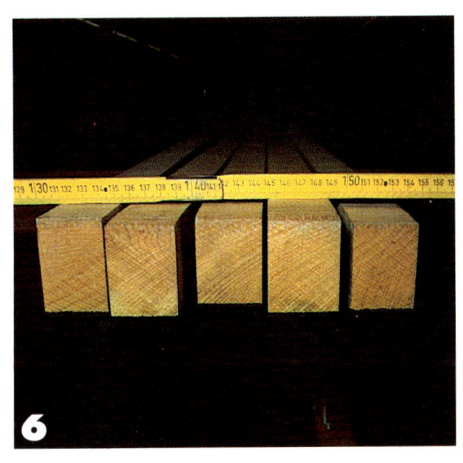

There is only one basic point that must be observed: the strips will only bend so far and the wider the strip the more difficult it is to bend. Should the hull 'belly' strongly as is the case with some IOR designs, then the strips should be laid parallel to the superstructure. In our case, a trial bend showed that the deck edge was not too curved to allow us to lay a strip along it. When the layout has been decided on then the drawing can start. This can be done by using a small cardboard template of the same width as a teak strip and about 40 centimetres long. The lines are drawn with a thick felt-tipped pen. Our first one was parallel to the toerail and the width of the template away from it, and all subsequent lines were drawn the same distance apart. If you subdivide the deck in this way you can see exactly where the butts will come later and how broad the framing strips around the superstructure will have to be. You can also see in advance how the planking around the hatch and the chain locker will look and get a picture in your mind's eye of the finished deck. Usually it's enough if you subdivide one half of the deck using that template, but take care – not all yachts are built absolutely symmetrically. A check of the measurements is a good idea.

While the planning was being done, suitable teak was being selected in the carpenter's shop at the boatyard and prepared for machining. Teak deck strips must always be cut from the trunk in such a way that seen from the ends of the strip, the annual rings are as near as possible perpendicular to avoid the wood warping when the deck gets wet later. If the rings are perpendicular, it expands only transversely and the deck remains flat. The teak trunk is first cut into planks, stored for a time, and then cut into strips. Truing follows and finally the tongue is milled. When all the strips have been finished, the unusable ones which have knot holes are picked out. If at all possible, the length of the strips should be at least two-thirds of that of the boat so that you don't have to have more than one end joint per strip. This will also allow you to spread the end joints over the deck so they don't show up so much.

10 The most important tool for our enterprise. A standard commercial electric drill has a length of plastic tubing fitted over the bit, which is indispensable as a hole-depth limiter.

11 The plug drill simultaneously drills both the hole for the screw and for the teak plug. Care must be taken to remove the chips after every operation.

12 The set of tools – to be found in most home tool boxes: screwdriver, folding rule, soft pencil, rasp, chisel, hand plane. It is important, however, to use only high-quality tools.

13 The first job on deck. Using a template, the lines for the strips are drawn; always parallel to the deck edge. Next comes the framing strip along the superstructure. The first strips must run through from stem to stern so as to produce a fair line. The work done here must be especially precise.

14 A short transverse piece, with mitred corners, forms the end at the stern. The first butt is arranged to take one-third of the strip width.

15 The joint in the framing strip at the corner of the superstructure. The gap between the mitred faces must be exactly the same width as the seam between adjoining strips. The holes should be about 1.5 strip widths from the ends.

16 The end joint between two strips: first, they are screwed down in direct contact, then the (tongue-width) seam is marked on them and the groove chiselled out.

17 The chainplate for the shrouds is fitted in. The plastic portion is later ground level with the disc sander and covered with a steel plate.

18 In the case of the guardrail stanchion feet, the strips are first left a bit long and screwed down. Then a line is drawn parallel to the edge of the foot and the strips sawn to the right length.

125

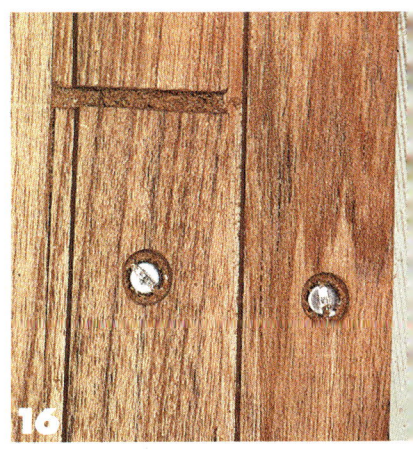

The first strip determines the line

In our case the first strip, which should be fastened firmly to the deck, was the fourth from outboard because this ran uninterrupted from bow to stern. That is particularly important because it is the only way to get the strip down without producing a wiggly line. It is essential that this first strip runs in a fair line, because all the others are aligned to it to the nearest millimetre. If you don't get that first one right, you've produced an element of error for all those that follow. The strip fasteners are 4.2 mm × 13 mm self-tapping steel screws, which are spaced 30 centimetres apart. The first strip should be fastened down using every screw but for the later ones, alternate screws are sufficient. But all necessary holes must be drilled because later, when bedding-in the strips, drilling is no longer possible.

After the fair-line strip, the framing strips around the superstructure are screwed down, again at 30 centimetre intervals. The corner joints are mitred, leaving a tongue-width gap, and the external angles at the superstructure get small, rounded inserts again leaving a gap. All these gaps must be the same size, otherwise the seam of black sealing compound applied later looks ugly.

The first butt

Now for the first butt. As can be seen from the illustrations, an appropriate part of the framing strip is cut away. First mark out and then drill the corner, then cut away the wedge with a chisel. This job needs a lot of practice and you have to be very careful with the first butt because, depending on the run of the grain, the framing strip is easily split and all the earlier work is wasted. Importantly, the length of the butt cut away must be matched exactly to the angle of the butting strip. Here it is essential to work to the nearest millimetre if the end result is to look good. If the two don't quite match, that is, the gap isn't parallel, you can cut a bit off and have another go with the plane to get the angle right – the strip is not wasted by any

19 Marking out the butt: the set square is held square to the laid strips and a line drawn on the king plank. All butts should be the same depth; one-third the width of a strip.

20 First produce the rounded corner of the butt using a plug drill, then shape the leading edge with a chisel. Take care not to split the wood.

21 The wood to be removed is first chiselled away roughly. Never use the chisel as a lever but pare the wood away downwards, and watch the grain!

22 After the rough cut, work back precisely to the pencil line. The corner must have dead straight lines; you can't do anything about it later if you go wrong.

23 When you've finished the butt, the strip is shaped to match. Keeping the gap width exactly right is important; even the radius must match.

24 It can happen that a butt gets mixed up with a framing strip fastening – not something you can anticipate. Here we've just got away with it. If need be, move the screw and plug the hole. But use a well-fitting plug and glue it in or it will look untidy.

25 When screwing the strips down they have to be absolutely parallel to give you the right seam width later on. This can easily be done correctly using wedges.

26 Where butts are very long around the superstructure you finally re-cut the edge with a chisel. The thin sliver is easily removed.

27 The corner joint at the superstructure where the strips get progressively shorter. The last one has to be made the right width too, to leave the right size seam. A short, handy strip of wood exactly the same width as the seam is used to get it just right.

127

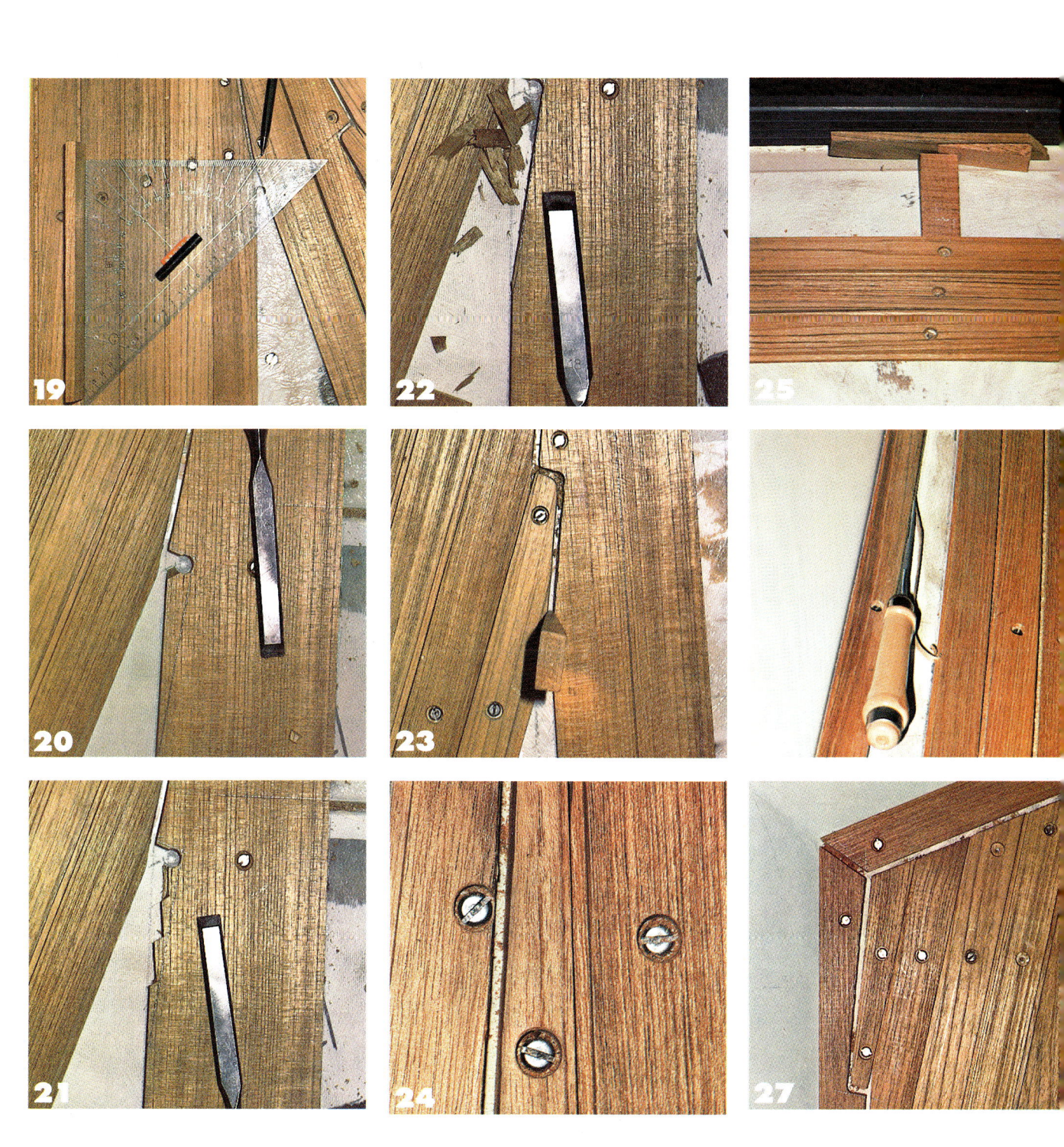

means. When screwing the strips down in the curved region, a considerable amount of force is often needed to get a strip parallel to its neighbour.

It is advisable to ask someone to hold the strip in place during drilling and screwing-down. Since the strips are not long enough individually to extend the full length of the deck, you will have some end joints. Here you also need a standard-width gap between adjoining ends; in practice you screw them down closer together and then open up the gap with a chisel.

When you have covered the whole deck with strips in this way and all work on the wood has been completed, the strips are numbered and taken up again. But don't just pile them all in one great heap; separate them into small batches to avoid the need for a mammoth search later on. This is particularly important because in the next

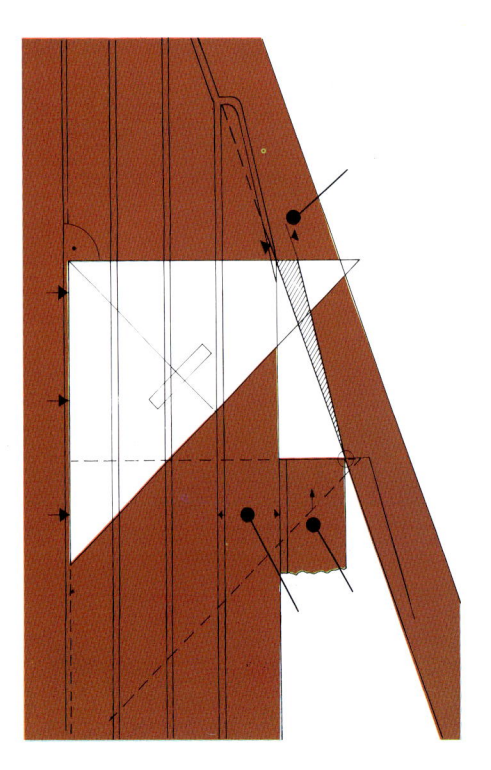

28 It is most important when laying the strips that they run in a fair curve. Initially leave about 1 metre between screws; the natural stress in the wood will help to get the curvature right. Later, insert all the screws.

29 Lay the superstructure framing strip so that there is a gap between it and the structure about the same width as the seam between the strips.

30 Always stagger the end joints between strips. This shows the minimum stagger; more is better because this makes the overall appearance much more balanced and un-fussy.

31 View of the deck: you start forward with the king plank which is screwed down precisely in the centre. The strips are then worked into this from both sides.

32, 33, 34 Each of the illustrations shows what you can hope to achieve in an eight-hour working day. At the end of the eight hours you are always surprised at how little has been achieved, but the short strips take a lot of time because they have to be fitted in at both ends. Rushing that work doesn't pay; you can't correct untidy butts later.

35 On the fifth day the forward part of the deck was finished.

36 When you have covered the entire deck with strips 'dry', they are all numbered in pencil and taken up again. If you're short of storage space you can do this separately for each half (store the strips systematically, not all mixed up!) and prime them before putting them down again.

The drawing shows how the individual butts are drawn. A short length of strip (A) marks the point where the angle starts. Butt length, width and contact angle determine the shape.

128

129

phase you are working against the clock with the sealant. This keeps soft (about the consistency of thick honey) for some two to three hours. 'Working' here means stirring-in the hardener, applying the paste using a sawtooth spatula and screwing down the strips into the sealant. In order to obtain good adhesion, the deck and the undersides of the strips have to be primed just before laying. If at all possible, this work should also be shared by two people: one to press the strips into position, the other to screw them down. Be prepared for that black mass to follow you everywhere, starting with the fingers and travelling up to the elbows! So have a good supply of old rags handy and wear your oldest clothes – disposable ones.

After all the strips have been replaced it's best not to do anything for a few days to let the sealant harden. The next task is plugging the screw holes, in our case some 1200. We stuck the plugs in with waterproof glue, so ensuring they would not fall out again in a hurry. This is extra work but worthwhile. A day later, the plugs can be cut off level with the deck using a handsaw – safer than using a chisel which could break the plug below deck level. You should use a chisel only in tight corners where access with a saw is not possible, and then only very carefully: first leave three millimetres or so proud, then pare down to the right length.

Priming and sealing seams

The next work phases are the priming and sealing of the seams, all of which are carefully coated with primer using a small, flat paint brush. When sealing the seams we didn't work with a gun; instead we took the paste straight from the tin and pressed it into the seams with a spatula. Where decks are already quite smooth this method has advantages. You start by pouring sealant into the seams over a small area. When you've done that and there are no air bubbles in the seams, pour the rest of the tin over that part of the deck and then use the spatula to spread it, working along the line of the strips; picking up surplus with the spatula and spreading it further. Next day, the places where air was

37 The 'chemicals' we need: primer for teak and GRP, plus the sealant paste with its hardener. Only by careful priming can proper bonding be assured.

38 The sealant paste with the hardener mixed-in. Using a stout wooden sawtooth spatula, the sealant paste is spread over the deck.

39 Stop paste getting on to GRP edges/surfaces by covering them with masking tape beforehand.

40 Never put more paste down on the deck than you can deal with in about two hours. If you're working by yourself, stir hardener into only one tin at a time and use that up. Screw the strips down into the soft paste.

41 If the paste has been applied too thickly, the strips will squeeze it out into the seams. Try to avoid that happening, because it prevents priming of the strip sides from above later.

42 All the strips have been screwed down, now you can start making the teak plugs – 1200 or so. Cut them out from battens, across the grain.

43 When cutting out, take care that a plug doesn't tear off from the batten as you withdraw the drill and remain stuck in it.

44 Before inserting the plugs, squeeze some waterproof glue into the holes which will ensure that they stay in. This is easily done with a squirter bottle.

131

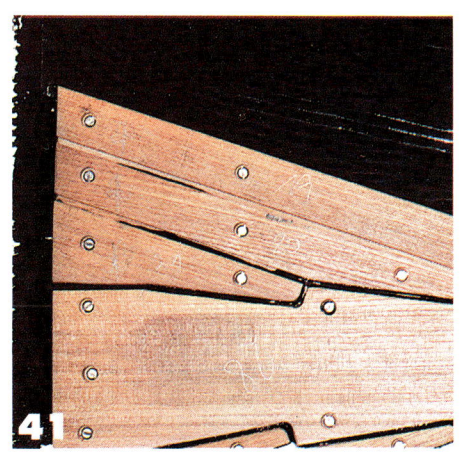

trapped will show up; you just make them good using the spatula. The deck is now pitch-black and anything but pretty. The sealant paste must now be allowed to harden thoroughly before being sanded down. Seven to ten days should be allowed. High atmospheric humidity accelerates hardening.

Sanding is the final process that crowns our enterprise – at last we can see something that looks like a teak deck. The sensible thing is to use a belt sander for this work, because that gives you the maximum effect and the belts have an acceptable working life. For corners and angles it may be worthwhile using the sanding disc in the drill; where even that is too big you will have to sand by hand. One working day is about what you need for sanding, and you need another for the finishing work – especially removing the masking tape protecting the superstructure, and polishing the GRP parts which, in spite of the greatest of care, will probably have black splashes.

Day-based work plan

Day		Hours
1	Old deck covering removed, deck polished with sander	8
2	Deck fittings removed and strips marked out	5
3	Electric drill converted, framing strips screwed down	8
4	First to sixth strip laid	8
5	Finished laying port side	8
6	Started around chain locker	5
7	Laid fore part	8
8	Finished fore part and chain locker	8
9	All strips laid except for fine details	8
10	All work with wood finished	5
11	Deck numbered and strips partially screwed down	3
12	All strips taken up again and two glued down	8
13	Finished gluing port side	9
14	Finished gluing starboard side	10
15	1200 plugs cut and glued-in	10
16	All seams primed and sealed	9
17	Seams topped up	4
18	Sanded deck (three sanders)	10
19	Finished sanding and removed tape	9
20	Fiddly work, cleaning and polishing	8
	Total	155

45 When inserting the plug, check that the grain runs exactly as that in the strip. Once you have fitted it, break free the rest of the batten.

46 Twelve hundred plugs have been inserted in the deck. One day later the ends can be sawn off. Check again that every screw hole has its plug.

47 If you proceed very carefully, you can cut the projecting ends off with a chisel. Check the run of the grain to avoid the break going too far down.

48 It's less risky, even if a bit slower, with a handsaw. The end is then smoothed with a sanding block.

49 Before applying the sealant paste to the seams, the deck should have been made as smooth as possible; that makes it easier to spread the paste. When sealing, check that you don't get air trapped in the seams. If you do get air bubbles, puncture them and top up with paste.

50 After some ten days, the sealant paste has hardened really thoroughly. Now you can start sanding and you will find that a belt sander is easiest.

51 When you've finished sanding – it will take about two days – the masking tape is removed from the superstructure and the nooks and crannies are sanded manually.

52 After the general clean up the GRP superstructure is polished with a special paste obtainable from good chandlers. Even elderly GRP can be made to look almost like new with this.

45
46
47
48
49
50
51
52

53 Final stage: the fittings are replaced.

Index

accumulator 49
angle grinder 19

basins 47, 49, 72
battens
   fitting 77–80, 81–97
   corner 117
   profiled 22–5
bevelled milling cutter 21
bunks 64–70

cabin, working in 16–21
cable cross sections 103–4
cable systems, electrical 103
Carl Beyer designs 11–15
carpets, fitted 110–11
CB-33 11–15
chainplate, covering 42
chart table 51
choosing a boat 8–15
circular saw 78
compression joint 87
cooker installation 58, 60, 63
corner post, galley 57
countersinking 19, 26–8
craft knife 21
crockery stowage 58, 61, 62, 63, 65
curved frames 38–40
cutlery stowage 58, 62, 63
cylindrical milling cutter 21

decking, laid teak 121–32
decorative strips 24
door frame 75
diamond wheel 19
disc grinder 19
distribution board 104–5
doors and frames 29–32
doors, Perspex 112–13
drains 47
drawing instruments 21
drills, electric 19

edging strips 24
electrical system 103–5
   wiring 49
engine soundproofing 101–2

finger-ring collars 25
fitted carpets 110–11
flooring 63
fresh water system 46–50

gas installation 86–90
grab handles 40, 63
grinding head 19
GRP sandwich construction 43
galley, fitting out 57–63

handles 25
handrails 25, 116
headlinings 37, 43–5, 81–97, 115
heads, fitting out 71–6
holes saw 19
hoses 49

instruments, installing 95–8
instrument locker 54
interior linings 33–7

jig saw 19
joins, covering 77–80

lightning conductor, fitting a 99–100
linings, interior 33–7
locker, chart 51–6

milling cutters 21
mitre jig 21

plugging 26–8
plug hole drill 19, 27
plugs 26, 79
   home made 27
priming and sealing seams 130–1
profiles 40
pumps, water 46–7

refrigerator 57, 58, 59, 62
round bars 24

sails, selecting 118–20
saloon 64–70
screw clamps 21
screwdrivers, electric 19

screws 27
scissors 21
seacock 49
sheet vinyl 33–4
size of boat 8
speedometer 95
spirit level 21
spring catches 29–32

tables 64–70
table, chart 51–6
tanks, water 46–7, 50
taps 49
teak rubbing strake 23

temporary floor 21
tools 17–21
treadboards 24

upholstery 91–4

varnishing 106–9
vinyl sheeting 33–4

window frames, wooden 25
wood cladding 43–5
work bench 21
workshop 21

Other titles available from Adlard Coles Nautical

☐	Boat Electrical Systems	£12.99
☐	Start With a Hull	£14.99
☐	The Fibreglass Boat Repair Manual	£19.99
☐	The Compleat Book of Yacht Care	£22.00
☐	Osmosis and the Care and Repair of Glassfibre Yachts	£11.99
☐	The Care and Repair of Small Marine Diesels	£9.99
☐	Boat Owner's Mechanical and Electrical Manual	£30.00
☐	Laying Up Your Boat	£7.99
☐	How to Design a Boat	£7.99

All these books are available or can be ordered from your local bookshop or can be ordered direct from the publisher. Simply tick the titles you want and fill in the form below.

Prices and availability subject to change without notice

Adlard Coles Nautical Cash Sales, PO Box 11, Falmouth, Cornwall.

Please send a cheque or postal order for the value of the book and add the following for postage and packing.

UK including the BFPO: £1.00 for one book plus 50p for the second book and 30p for each additional book ordered, up to a £3.00 maximum.

OVERSEAS including EIRE: £2.00 for the first book, plus £1.00 for the second book, and 50p for each additional book ordered.

OR Please debit this amount from my Access/Visa Card (delete as appropriate).

Card number ☐☐☐☐☐☐☐☐☐☐☐☐

Amount £ ....

Expiry date ....

Signed ....

Name ....

Address ....

Fax no: 0326 376423